ANTIQUE MAPS AND CHARTS

ANTIQUE MAPS AND CHARTS

A. L. HUMPHREYS

INTRODUCTION BY
JONATHAN POTTER

BRACKEN BOOKS
LONDON

Previously published as *Old Decorative Maps and Charts* in 1926 by
Halton & Truscott Smith Ltd., London and
Minton, Balch & Company, New York

This edition published 1989 by Bracken Books
an imprint of Bestseller Publications Ltd.
Princess House, 50 Eastcastle Street
London W1N 7AP, England

ISBN 1 85170 256 3

Printed and bound in Hong Kong

CONTENTS

LIST OF BLACK AND WHITE PLATES

The Sea Coasts of South America. (Linschoten, 'Navigatio, etc.,' 1599)
North-East Africa, Arabia, Persia and India. (Linschoten, 'Navigatio, etc.,' 1599)
Britain at the time of the Saxon Heptarchy. (Speed, 'The Theatre of the Empire of Great Britain,' 1611)
Middlesex, with the Cities of London and Westminster. (Speed, 'Theatre of the Empire, etc.,' 1611)
The County of Surrey. (Speed, 'Theatre of the Empire, etc.,' 1611)
Cambridgeshire. (Speed, 'Theatre of the Empire, etc.,' 1611)
The Indian Archipelago. (Mercator's Atlas, 1633)
Japan. (Mercator's Atlas, 1633)
Virginia and Florida. (Mercator's Atlas, 1633)
The Islands of Cuba and Hispaniola (Hayti). (Mercator's Atlas, 1633)
The Kingdoms of Fez and Morocco. (Mercator's English Atlas, 1636)
China. (Mercator's English Atlas, 1636)
New England. (Mercator, 'Historia Mundi,' 1635)
Virginia. (Mercator, 'Hist. Mundi,' 1635)
Valois. (Blaeu, 'Nieuwe Atlas,' 1642-3)
The Territory of Frankfort on the Main. (Blaeu, 'Nieuwe Atlas,' 1642-3)
North and South America. (Blaeu, 'Nieuwe Atlas,' 1642-3)
The Straits of Magellan and Tierra del Fuego. (Blaeu, 'Nieuwe Atlas,' 1642-3)
New Belgium and New England. (Blaeu, 'Nieuwe Atlas,' 1642-3)
Brazil. (Blaeu, 'Nieuwe Atlas,' 1642-3)
Chart of the Coast of Guiana. (Dudley, 'Dell' Arcano del Mare,' 1646-7)
Old and New Virginia. (Dudley, 'Dell' Arcano del Mare,' 1646-7)
The County of Essex. (Jansson, 'Novus Atlas,' 1658)
The South Polar Regions. (Jansson, 'Novus Atlas,' 1658)
Chart of the North Atlantic. (Jansson, 'Novus Atlas,' 1658)
Title Page to Pieter Goos, 'Zee-Atlas,' 1666
Chart of the Sea Coast of Russia, Lapland, etc. (Seller, 'The English Pilot,' 1671-5)
Chart of the Coast of Guinea. (Van Keulen, 'Sea Atlas,' 1682)

ILLUSTRATIONS IN THE TEXT

LIST OF COLOUR PLATES

PUBLISHER'S NOTE

Unless indicated otherwise all map sizes are folio (i.e. approximately 21 × 16ins.) and are measured width by height.

Please note that the original introduction is reproduced here; it includes reference to prices in old currency (pounds, shillings and pence).

INTRODUCTION

On first considerations the collecting of ancient maps may appear to be a relatively recent phenomena – just one more of those fields of 'collectables' which have been marketed in the last ten to fifteen years with an eye to their 'investment' potential, ranking with many other, rather dubious, categories deemed worthy of study and purchase, particularly, by those who want to sell them. This, however, is not the case. Maps and atlases have been collected and appreciated over hundreds of years by those with an interest in the history, romance and artistry which are combined in many maps produced in manuscript or, from the late fifteenth century, in printed form.

Although cartographic productions of today may appear 'unpicturesque' when compared with some of the ornate words of the seventeenth century, for instance, there is no denying the skill of the designers and draftsmen who have worked together to produce a detailed representation of an area if for greater accuracy and detail than could ever be seen in a photograph of equivalent scale.

The appreciation of maps has been recorded throughout history as being enjoyed by monarchs, politicians, academics, merchants and military figures – in short, virtually anyone who could read. Furthermore maps, as practical working tools, have occupied a position of immense influence in each of these afore-mentioned categories and reflect on examination, the history of man's knowledge of the world, of nations' relationships with each other, and, the changing physical appearance of our planet – whether ataclysmic in the form of earthquake, flood or volcano, or gradual, such as climatic, erosive or man-influenced.

The literature available to students of the history of cartography is now extensive ranging from the most general introduction to the subject either for the potential collector of maps, or, by way of discussions of early surveying and printing methods, for the student of technical aspects of printed map making. To support this there are numerous other works which concentrate solely on the mapping of specific areas, by individual mapmakers, or even on particular maps. Many of these more detailed works are available only in obscure scientific papers and journals and, as such, require a great deal of hard work in being able to locate, let alone read.

Against such a background large amounts of information are now available for the student. Sixty years ago the situation was markedly different

– although many specialized papers had been produced there were virtually no books catering to general interest readers who might wish to see illustrations of old maps and satisfy their curiosity about the whole field of mapmaking in the early centuries of printing. Arthur L Humphrey's *Old Decorative Maps and Charts* first published in 1926, albeit in an edition of fifteen hundred copies, was amongst the first books to cater for a market which has become now, so popular.

Since 1926 Humphrey's book has been reprinted and revised in a number of different editions – each of them, after a relatively short period in print becoming sought-after collector's items. Bracken Books, in reprinting the original introduction, the majority of Humphrey's plates and up-dating the list of reference works, make available, once again, a fine book recently only available to bibliophiles in antiquarian bookseller's shops and catalogues.

Humphrey's book was a celebration of the fascination of old maps and, in particular, those maps in the collection of Mr A.G.H. Macpherson. Macpherson was a book and map collector and member of the Society for National Research. During the early years of this century he built up one of the most spectacular collections of maps and atlases ever held in private hands – a list of over two hundred and fifty books and atlases in the collection includes one, or more, copies of all major printed atlases published since the 1480s (some twenty different editions of Abraham Ortekius' 'Theatrum Orbis Terrarum' – generally acknowledged as the first printed atlas – are listed). To assemble such a collection of atlases now would not be impossible but would involve enormous patience and, at today's prices (never mind tomorrow's), assuming all items were to become available, would probably require an investment in the region of one-and-a-half to two million pounds. Humphrey's original introduction gives an interesting clue as to prices then – a Blaeu atlas at £320, a Goos atlas at £70, Saxton at £188 – today's prices would be, respectively, around £100,000, £20,000 and £50,000.

The importance of this collection was such that it was ultimately purchased for, and formed the nucleus of the magnificent collection of maps and atlases now housed at the National Maritime Museum at Greenwich on the Thames. In 1927 Macpherson's collection, including also maritime paintings, drawings, ship models and navigational instruments, was offered for sale at £108,000. The Society for National Research had stated, in 1910, one of its major aims was the establishment of a national maritime museum.

Although Royal assent for such a foundation was not granted till 1934, the shipping magnate Sir James Aird, also a member of the Society for National Research, saw the importance of such an unique collection and had funded its acquisition in 1927. Within a few years and a number of subsequent purchases the National Maritime Museum quickly established itself one of the world's great libraries of cartographical items – maps, atlases and globes.

Humphrey's original introduction not only gives an interesting background to the development of the map business prior to the 'modern' developments of the nineteenth century but also conveys his own excitement at examining such a collection of atlases. The map enthusiast gains much enjoyment from looking at a map with an understanding of some of the problems and difficulties which may have been encountered by the sixteenth century navigator who voyaged to places unknown and reprinted them to the mapmakers in Europe who drew, engraved, printed, coloured and bound these records of the known state of the world.

The antiquarian map business since the 1920s has changed emphasis dramatically and this is illustrated clearly by the large number of books now available for map collectors. When Macpherson built his collection the availability of most of the major atlases could be taken for granted. Most of the better stocked antiquarian booksellers in Britain, Europe and North America who dealt in travel and topography subjects could be expected to have good examples of atlases which are now only rarely available on the market. Those booksellers might also be expected to have a stock of loose sheet maps – either originally issued individually or in atlas form and subsequently removed from their binding.

Nowadays few examples for the great atlases come onto the market anywhere in the world although there are specialist mapsellers who cater for the large business in original maps for collectors and decorators; larger and more comprehensive stocks of these are now available since so many atlases, over the last fifty or sixty years, may be imperfect, lacking sheets and damaged, have been 'broken' to satisfy market demands.

Jonathan Potter
January 1989

IT would have been strange if the charm and great decorative value of old maps had not in this beauty loving age become revealed to collectors both in England and in America. The wonder is indeed that the hand-coloured maps, of the seventeenth century especially, have lain for so long buried away in libraries. For generations old maps were ill treated and disregarded because it pleased everyone to think that a new map would always displace an earlier one. Perhaps no class of printed matter has been destroyed as much as have early maps. A change has now taken place in our regard for maps and the enthusiasm of collectors has come to the rescue of them. We all now see that in old maps may be found a new source for intelligent enjoyment. Not only the great atlases of the seventeenth century, but single maps as well are being sought for and hunted down both for the story of exploration and discovery and for their beauty of ornamentation, their rich colouring, their bits of costume and heraldry and the amount of very evident soul which their designers and engravers put into their execution. The collection of rare atlases and maps formed by Mr. A. G. H. Macpherson has been placed at my disposal and this has enabled me in writing this book to have under my eyes some of the finest atlases and maps in existence. Mr. Macpherson's Collection forms the basis of this historical study of old decorative maps and charts.

As he stood on the shore and gazed out on the horizon, we have but faint and dim notions of what primitive man's ideas of the world may have been before there were any maps to guide him, even of the most fanciful and fantastic design. No doubt but that he regarded the heavens as the roof of his habitation, and if in his scheme of things he considered an infernal world at all he thought of it as extending beneath the waters of the sea. That was enough to satisfy his limited yearnings.

Astronomy we know played a very important part in the work and in the speculations of the earliest geographers, but even in the dim and remote past there must have been a feeling of wonderment at the sun, the moon and the stars which would have started curiosity in the minds of those who were slowly becoming conscious of the marvels of the world in which they were living. The Phœnicians were the great maritime nation of antiquity. They traversed the shores of the Mediterranean and came as far as the coasts of Britain. They acted as carriers for the Egyptians, sending ships to the Red Sea and coasting the Arabian Peninsula. They were an expansive race, but they probably kept much of their store of geographical knowledge to themselves. They were great navigators. It is to the navigating races that we must look first for maps and charts.*

To Herodotus belongs the distinction of making a reference to what must have been a primitive if not the earliest map. Herodotus was keenly observant and gleaned more than anyone as he travelled. Strabo says that Anaximander, who was born B.C. 612, was the first who represented the world upon a map, but there is a passage in Herodotus which is more definite than the one in Strabo. Herodotus says that Aristagoras, when he went to Cleomenes the King of Sparta to induce him to invade Persia, produced before the Spartan King "a bronze tablet upon which the whole circuit of the earth was engraved with all its seas and rivers." It is in this passage from Herodotus that a map or the equivalent of it is named in literature for the first time. From early classical literature we may treasure up such scattered references as exist to map lore. Claudius Aelianus, a gossiping bachelor writer, whose *Variæ Historiæ* are filled with anecdotes, relates that Socrates in his wisdom, in order to check some symptoms of swelled head in Alcibiades regarding what he boastfully considered his large estates, brought him to a place where a map of the world was exhibited and rather witheringly asked him to point out on it where his estates were situated. Theophrastus, the favourite pupil of Aristotle, and who inherited his library and manuscripts, bequeathed a portico in the neighbourhood of the Lyceum at Athens for the suspension of a map of the world. Although Strabo, the grand old man of early geography, gives some meagre rules for the drawing of maps, there are very few and scanty early references to cartography. Map science in the ancient world was in a miserable state. The writers of the period who were, as far as geography went, armchair philosophers, sat still and dreamed dreams and worked out theoretical schemes. They had no gift or inclination or knowledge sufficient to produce anything that could be termed a map.

What the earliest maps were we do not definitely know, but we can form a reasonable conjecture. The earth at that time was supposed to be a flat circular plain, or disc, the broadest part

*Keane, *Evolution of Geography*, p 4.

being from east to west, which was entirely surrounded by an ocean, or great river, that washed it upon all sides. In about the centre of this plain, Greece was supposed to be situated. The great central sea of the inhabited region was the Mediterranean. The farthest point known to the west was the Straits of Gibraltar, then called the Pillars of Hercules. The southern part comprised the north of Africa as far as the deserts; whilst the region north embraced the countries bordering upon the Mediterranean, and an unknown hyperborean land farther to the north, with the Euxine and Caspian Seas at the north-east. The farthest eastern point known was about the western limit of India. This was what would then be contained in a map as a representation of the earth. The sun was supposed to pass under and around this flat plain, which was then the mode of accounting for the changes of day and night. The space beneath was supposed to be a great vault, called Tartarus, the abode of the spirits of the wicked among men, as the region corresponding to it, above the plain, was the heaven, or abode of the gods. The unknown region beyond the Pillars of Hercules was filled up with creations of the fertile imagination of the Greeks. To the north-west and north were the Cimmerians, a people living in perpetual darkness; and the Hyperboreans, a race supposed to be exempt from toil, disease or wars, who enjoyed life for a thousand years in a state of undisturbed serenity. To the west of Sicily were the enchanted islands of Circe and Calypso, and the floating islands of Eolus. A little to the north of the Pillars of Hercules was the entrance to the infernal regions, and far out in the Western Ocean, beyond the limits of the known earth, was the happy region called Elysium, a land of perpetual summer, where a gentle zephyr constantly blew; where tempests were unknown; and where the spirits of those whose lives had been approved by the gods dwelt in perpetual felicity. Here also were the gardens of the Hesperides, with their golden apples guarded by the singing nymphs, who dwelt on the river Oceanus, which was in the extreme west, and the position of which was constantly shifted as geographical knowledge increased. No doubt, the unknown and fabulous was mingled with what was known in the map of Hacatæus.*

Among the Egyptians, map making remained in its infantile stage, for the Egyptians had no geographical knowledge derived from actual travel, but their knowledge of astronomy came to

* Daly, *History of Early Cartography.*

their aid. It was from the Greeks really that map making obtained its scientific development. Anaximander, a pupil of Thales, is believed to have been the first to determine the compass of the earth and the sea. Eratosthenes, the keeper of the Alexandrian Library, successfully combined the offices of geographer and astronomer. He collected the entire geographical knowledge of his time and such portions as exist are found embodied in the works of Strabo.*

To Marinus of Tyre a very important place must be given in the early history of maps. Marinus was a Greek geographer who flourished about A.D. 150. He was the founder of scientific geography. Marinus assigned to each place its latitude or longitude. Although his work is lost we know that it was upon his research and discoveries that Ptolemy put together his great book. Ptolemy laboured under many dazzling delusions, yet he was the first to realise and describe the extent of the surface of the globe.

It has been said that the Greeks measured the earth by the stars and the Romans by milestones. By the Romans a map was used as a means of getting from place to place. They regarded maps entirely from the utilitarian point of view. The Romans when making a map blotted out everything that did not appertain to the places where they were directing their forces. They otherwise acted as the lords of creation. With the exception of Julius Cæsar the Romans were deficient in great geographers. Their dealings were with milestones and itineraries. Yet Agrippa prepared a famous map of the world and had it set up in Rome for public view and reference in order that the youth of the great empire might see their inheritance. This same idea of placing maps in public places was carried on for many centuries and as late as the fifteenth century Fra Mauro painted a map on the wall of a convent at Venice which must have been an admirable production, remarkable for the extent of the geographical information it embodied and the artistic skill with which it was executed. To return for a moment to Roman maps, the only map of the imperial epoch which has come down to us is the Tabula Peutingeriana or the Itinerarium of Castorius, which takes its modern name from Conrad Peutinger of Augsburg who possessed it in the sixteenth century. It is now preserved in the Imperial Library of Vienna. It goes back to the third century, though the actual copy in Vienna is not older than the seven-

* Keane, p. 5.

teenth century. It consists of twelve folio sheets of parchment which originally formed one long strip. Various facsimiles of it have been issued. Although mediævalised, there is no question that it is a map of the pagan world, a genuine touchstone of ancient geography, which honour it shares with the great work of Ptolemy. It is drawn in an elongated form similar in shape to the Bayeux tapestry and in it are laid down not only the roads of the empire, but also three classes of illustrations. The smaller towns are depicted by little houses, the greater ones such as Rome by vignettes or medallions, and forests are represented by trees.*

In the middle of the sixth century a monk called Cosmas, who had originally been a travelling merchant and had journeyed as far as India and Ceylon, produced a map which represented no doubt the mediæval and ecclesiastical mind. He attempted to refute the idea that the world was a sphere. "If it be a sphere," said Cosmas, "then there must actually be people standing 'feet to feet' and he attempted to satisfy his followers by drawing a picture of four men standing 'feet to feet' which he thought was a sufficiently convincing *reductio ad absurdam*."† The disappearance of the sun was accounted for by Cosmas by the alleged presence of a huge mountain "in the north" behind which the sun went down, leaving the earth in darkness until the next morning. One of the most extravagant notions of early geographers was that the tides and the ebb and flow of the waters were caused by the breathings of a huge marine animal.

As early as the tenth century there are traces of Arabic influence upon map making, but the Arabs were more interested in astronomy in its connection with geography than they were with topography and map making as geographical science. We have Arabic maps of the tenth, eleventh and up to the fourteenth century, which show them to have been poor cartographers, and they produced the greatest confusion in their maps. Most of the Arabic geographers accepted the idea that the earth was a sphere. Edrisi, the most famous of the Arabian map makers, thought it was a globe floating in an ocean like an egg in a basin of water, and that it was the half that was above the surface that was inhabited. Whenever Edrisi had to refer to fabulous and impossible things asserted by his predecessors he accompanied the statement by a regular formula: "God only knows how this is." At the Atlantic he stops short, calling it "The Sea of Darkness." The earliest copy of Edrisi's map is in the Bodleian Library in a

* Beazley, *Dawn of Modern Geography*, I., 381-2. † Keane, p. 39.

fifteenth century manuscript and therefore of much later date than the original which was produced at the beginning of the twelfth century.

In all mediæval maps fancy filled in the blanks in the mental horizons of the map makers. The popular idea of the world was taken from priests and poets. The value of such maps from the geographical standpoint is *nil* and they are only of use as representing the mediæval and ecclesiastical mind which endeavoured to harmonise everything with the Bible. The high standard of Ptolemy and the legacy of world knowledge bequeathed by the Greeks and Romans did not fit in with monastic teaching. As early as the eighth century what are known as *mappæmondi* were in use. The earliest of these occurs in a manuscript in the Library of Albi in Languedoc and with all its errors it stands as the oldest geographical monument of Western Europe in the middle ages.* Its closest parallel is found in the Anglo-Saxon map of the tenth century in the British Museum. It presents a mixture of Biblical and classical geography in which the British Isles are represented woefully distorted. In the north-east corner is a drawing of a lion with the legend "Here are many lions." A taste for the fabulous produced marvellous results. Very notable is the famous ecclesiastical map of the world dating from the thirteenth century which is in Hereford Cathedral. It was drawn by Richard of Haldingham. It has the most strange symbolism and curious natural history in which the mermaid, the unicorn and the dragon are mixed up with the ape, the whale and the lion.† Stranger still are the marvellous headless men with eyes in their breasts, four-eyed Ethiopians and other monsters introduced in a series of pictures along the African coast. In one corner is a seated figure wearing a triple crown which is supposed to represent Julius Cæsar delivering a written order or warrant to three philosophers to survey the world. As a specimen of cartography it is very gross and exhibits the profoundest ignorance of the world in general, but an ignorance also of England and Scotland, countries with which it might be supposed the author would be familiar. Being drawn by an ecclesiastic, it is covered with religious conceptions such as a representation of the Garden of Eden, the expulsion of Adam and Eve, the Tower of Babel, the Apostles, Satan bearing off the condemned, and the favourite idea that Jerusalem was in the centre of the world. The Hereford map should be viewed as a literary monument on

* Beazley, I., 386. † Keane, p. 77.

which is registered the position of learning towards the close of the thirteenth century.

In the history of map making *mappæmondi* did not tend towards much progress or development. They lasted, it is true, for centuries, but left no mark on the modern map.* Later than the Hereford map, but still belonging to the same class is the map by Ralph Higden of the latter half of the fourteenth century, in which the legends of the Amazons and of the one-eyed Cyclops are retained. England is occupied by fourteen towns only and is coloured red, probably the earliest example of a coloured map. The sea in this map is also coloured green, except the Red Sea, which is painted bright red. Maps of this class were of little use to the mass of the populace at the time they were made and of little use to the learned, to whom they were only misleading by their fantastic emblems and symbols. They have no connection with improvement or development in cartography which soon after the end of the fourteenth century began to make considerable progress. The fathers of the church and the philosophers for several centuries after the time of Ptolemy took a deep interest in the study of geography which was carried on in the schools of Alexandria. At a similar school at Ravenna, too, great efforts were made in producing descriptive itineraries for pilgrims and others, but it took time for things to improve.

In the middle ages many factors caused the discrediting for a time of the influence of Ptolemy, and chief among these was the disposition of the clergy to test all geographical knowledge by the standard of the Bible, and as the Bible afforded no authority that the earth is a globe, all who maintained the sphericity of the earth were rejected. Cosmas, for instance, was typical of this ecclesiastical teaching and maintained that the earth was an oblong plain enclosed at its four extremities by huge walls of immense thickness on which the firmament or vault of the heavens rested. Cosmas drew his map accordingly.

The manuscript cloister maps of the Middle Ages with their scraps of learning borrowed from the manuals of superstitious teaching or from such books as Pliny and the Antonine Itinerary soon made way for the first real maps, which are known as Portolan charts and which date from the fourteenth century. Roman traders and navigators had what are known as *peripli,* which were of the nature of sailing directions and not maps. The Portolan charts about which I must now say something

* Andrews.

served much the same purpose as the *peripli* had done centuries earlier, although there is no reason to suppose that there was any direct connection or descent from the *peripli* to the Portolan chart.* The word "*periplus,*" used by the Greeks even to denote a harbour or sailing guide, was never applied to a sea-chart. The Portolan charts were the first scientifically constructed maps with decorative features and they came into being with the discovery of the magnet for geographical direction. There were three stages in magnet knowledge : (1) the discovery that the lode stone attracted iron; (2) the discovery that to steel or hardened iron could be imparted the attractive power of the lode stone; and (3) the discovery that the magnet or magnetised iron possessed the quality of indicating the north. It is this last discovery that revolutionised map production although master mariners would not for a long time steer by any instrument so like one of infernal make.† In addition to the magnet as of use to mariners, there were other causes for the vast improvement in map production in the fourteenth century. There were the pilgrim habit, the crusading impulse and the old Viking spirit which contributed much, but beyond these and by far the most potent of all were maritime enterprise and commercial activity in the Mediterranean affecting such places as Venice, Genoa, Pisa, Majorca, Barcelona and others. The pursuits of the Latin races of the Mediterranean were maritime. They were carriers by water of all products between Asia and Europe and they became what the Arabs never were, a great nautical race.‡ The Catalans engaged in navigation became noted for their Portolan charts. In 1375, Charles V. of France sent to the Catalan map makers to have a map of the world executed and the result was an atlas of six maps drawn on vellum and illuminated in colours. This famous map was reproduced in all the Mediterranean towns and ports for the use of mariners. Each master of a vessel (or pilot, as he was then called) had a copy of it and for a long time it was the map in use for all practical purposes.

Portolan charts multiplied rapidly when they had once come into being. They embodied the notes, plans and oral traditions of generations of pilots and captains. Nothing in the history of map making is more significant or more impressive than the passage from the pictured cloister maps of the dark ages to the great series of Catalan and Mediterranean charts. The Portolan chart was usually drawn on parchment, though in time paper

* Beazley, III., 528. † Beazley, III., 511. ‡ Daly, p. 28.

came to be used.* Sometimes they are found as single sheets or in sheets bound together as in an atlas. Many splendid examples now known have been preserved because they were specially made for Kings or patrons of the arts, and they were therefore preserved in great libraries. With a few exceptions they are all the work of Italian and Catalan chart makers. Herein we may see the leadership exercised by the seamen of the Italian and of the Eastern Iberian Peninsula, a leadership which began as early as the eleventh century and which continued until America had been discovered, Africa had been circumnavigated and the water route to the Indies had been made known.†

As Portolan charts were primarily intended for the use of seamen they therefore give fuller details of coast lines and islands than of interior regions. Their decorative value is considerable when they are found well preserved. Important towns were shewn on them by small pictures. Separate States have their names given and are sometimes distinguished by a coat-of-arms. Castile for example has the quartered field with the castle on a red ground and a red lion on a silver ground. Aragon has a red standard in a gold field, and Portuguese territory a banner having five dots in a blue field. Legends were often inserted where space permitted referring to the products of the country. Occasionally one finds features borrowed from the ecclesiastical and cloister maps which had gone before. Gog and Magog appear and fabulous islands are sometimes inserted. In the earliest Portolan charts colours were not much used, but as time went on the chart maker saw opportunities for displaying his sense of colour in banners, borders and labels in which to place the scale of miles.‡ Certain colours and conventional shapes were given to some islands. Thus Rhodes long after the Turkish conquest regularly appears in white with a black cross symbolic of the Hospitallers, while red or reddish brown is always kept for the Red Sea.§ In the Portolan chart of Petrus Roselli, dated 1468, the larger cities are distinguished by groups of turrets and banners, and while the Papal banner flies over Avignon those of Castile and Aragon mark Spain prominently. It is well known that Roman maps were oriented with the south at the top, an arrangement met with also in most Arabic maps. Maps of the early mediæval centuries have the East at the top. Portolan charts are nearly all oriented with the north at the top, an idea

* Beazley, III., 512. † E. L. Stevenson, *Portolans*, p. 17.
‡ E. L. Stevenson. § Beazley, III., 514.

which has since been adopted in maps since the discovery of the mariners' compass.*

The collector and student of the earliest manuscript maps will naturally be obliged for the most part to be satisfied with facsimiles, not that there are many good facsimiles for the use of collectors. Many of these even have become scarce. It is, however, a fortunate fact in the history of cartography that there have been diligent and wealthy students who have devoted their lives and their means to rescuing valuable manuscript maps and reproducing them in a worthy form. Between the years 1849 and 1852 the Vicomte de Santarem produced an atlas of great value in which were reproduced in folio size the earliest efforts of map makers from the sixth to the fifteenth centuries. Those reproductions included many of the earliest *mappæmondi* and Portolans. The whole book in four sections is a priceless contribution to early map history. The book is now very rare. Many years later there appeared a work of almost equal importance in Konrad Miller's "*Mappæmondi*" issued at Stuttgart in 1895-1898. This contains facsimiles on a smaller scale of most of the famous world maps of the middle ages, including the Anglo-Saxon map, the Hereford map and Higden's maps. Another standard work was Jomard's great book upon the monuments of geography. This contains some early itineraries as well as the *mappamondi* of Juan de la Cosa, the pilot of Columbus. It has as well the *mappamondi of* Sebastian Cabot.

Nordenskiöld's *Periplus* gives a large number of reproductions of old charts and maps. Besides dealing with early *peripli* and Greek and Roman cartography before Ptolemy it has a number of early maps in facsimile relating to America. Nordenskiöld's famous *Facsimile Atlas* deals largely with the revival of Ptolemy in the fifteenth century, but it omits by design to facsimile early manuscript maps. In 1879 Charles Daly contributed to the Journal of the American Geographical Society a lengthy article upon the early history of Cartography. This valuable article, into which is compressed the knowledge of a life time, contains illustrations, although much reduced in size, of a large number of the earliest conceptions of the world from the Greek maps up to the time of Mercator. No student of early geography can omit to pay tribute to the great work by C. Raymond Beazley, *The Dawn of Modern Geography*. Each of the three volumes of this work covers ground hardly touched

* E. L. Stevenson.

upon by any other book. In each of its three volumes there is a section dealing with the history of the maps and containing reproductions on a good scale of the earliest maps with historical notes and criticisms of the utmost value. There is as well a brief volume on the *Evolution of Geography* by John Keane, published in 1899. It deals with the rise and progress of geographical knowledge up to the time of the first great circumnavigators. Its chapter on " Early and Mediæval maps " has with it a number of illustrations including Greek and Arabic conceptions of the world *mappæmondi* and Portolans. The study of Portolans has within recent years greatly advanced, chiefly because of the special study given to them in Italy, but partly too from their significance, pointed out so definitely by Mr. Beazley, and equally also from the great assistance given to their study by the Hispanic Society of America. No praise could be sufficiently high for the work done by this wealthy Society in collecting early portolans and reproducing them magnificently in facsimile. Mr. E. Luther Stevenson, who has in recent years done so much valuable work for cartography through the Hispanic Society, notes that his Society possesses the largest collection of Portolan charts in America.

We have seen that towards the end of the fourteenth century the Catalan map produced by Charles V. of France marked something of an epoch in cartography. In the next century, *viz.* the fifteenth, great acquisitions were made to the knowledge of the world, principally by the results of the travels of Marco Polo. It was about the middle of the fifteenth century that a Carmelite friar, Fra Mauro, painted the map I have already referred to on the walls of a convent in Venice. This map embodied remarkable geographical information. It was a very successful achievement representing the whole earth within a circle. Following upon this map was the effort of another Italian, Toscanelli, a cosmographer of Florence, who inspired by the travels of Marco Polo sent his map to Columbus. It is this map of Toscanelli which is a landmark in a great age of discovery.

In a remarkable and memorable passage in Bryce's *Holy Roman Empire* he refers to the age of discovery and to one event to which the history of the world offers no parallel before or since —the discovery of America. Bryce speaks of the lifting of the cloud round the borders of civilization and the removal of the mysterious awe with which men had regarded the Earth, all of which vanished when astronomers and geographers taught them that she was an insignificant globe which, so far from being the centre of the universe, was herself swept round in the motion of one of the least of its countless systems.

The globular form of the Earth was at this time far from being generally accepted. Columbus himself believed that the Earth was of the shape of a pear. Among the most quaint ideas urged against Columbus's voyage was that if he ever succeeded in reaching the east by travelling west the rotundity of the globe would present a kind of mountain, up which it would be impossible for his vessel to sail! The discoveries of Columbus appear first in the map made by John Ruysch in the edition of Ptolemy's Atlas printed in Rome in 1508. Three years later, in 1511, Bernard Sylvanus produced an edition of Ptolemy with a map of the world on a heart shaped projection, and in this map America, under the name of "The Land of the Holy Cross," was set out more fully and accurately than in the map by Ruysch. In 1520 Peter Benewitz made a heart-shaped map after the method of Sylvanus and this has become famous as one of the first maps upon which the name of America appears. Simon Grynæus in 1531 published a map of the world which became for some time an authoritative map and was adopted by Sebastian Munster in his *Cosmography*, a book of wide popularity in the sixteenth century, with some early views of towns.

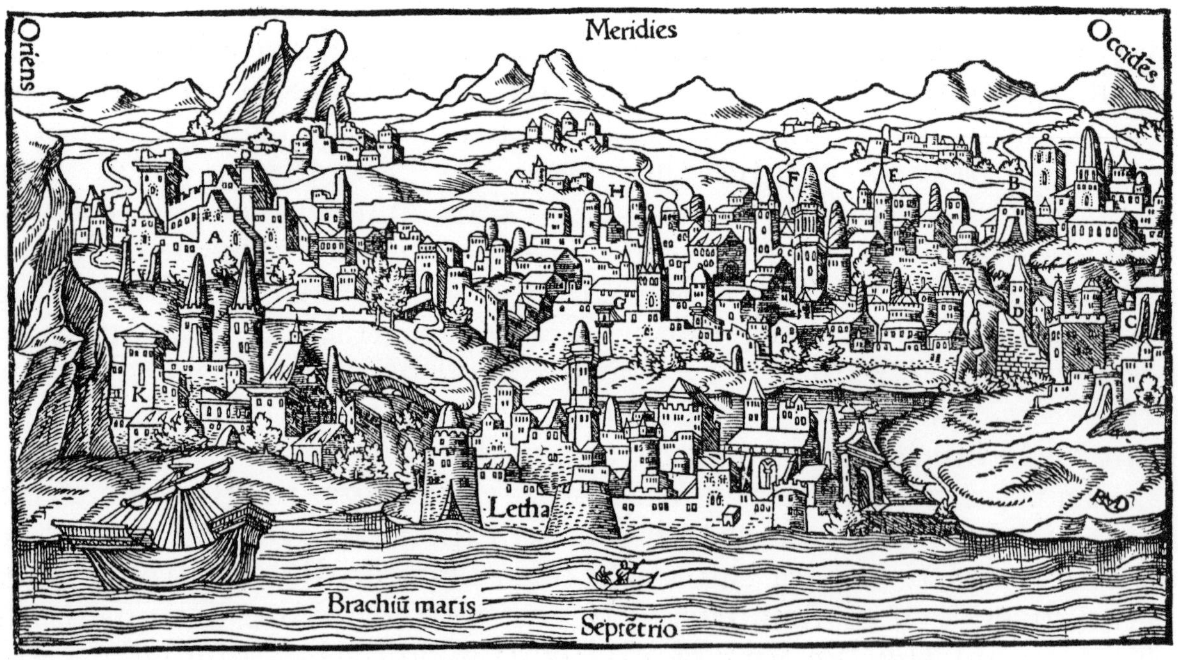

EDINBURGH. FROM SEBASTIAN MUNSTER'S COSMOGRAPHY, 1550.

A. *Palatium Regis.* B. *Arx puellarum.* C. *Ecclesia S. Cutberti.* D. *Ecclesia S. Egidii.* E. *Minoritæ.* F. *Ecclesia beatæ Mariæ in cāpo.* G. *Collegia reginæ.* H. *Prædicatores.* K. *Monasterium S. Crucis.*

The one great figure in early map history which stands out above all others is Ptolemy. Ptolemy has preserved for us all that was known of geography in the first centuries of our era. But it was not until Ptolemy's great work was translated into Latin in the early fifteenth century by Jacobus Angelus and first printed in 1475 that it began to exercise a dominating influence upon geographical ideas.* This revival of Ptolemy continued until the time of Mercator and Ortelius in the late sixteenth century. The maps in Ptolemy have been attributed to a draughtsman named Agathodæmon, whom some believe to have lived in the Byzantine period, but he more probably executed these maps under the Pagan Empire, if indeed he was not an alias for Ptolemy himself.†

Ptolemy attempted to set out the whole world upon scientific and astronomical principles. If his maps failed to meet with complete success it was not on account of a faulty method but from lack of accurate data.‡ It is generally recognised that Ptolemy derived much of his knowledge from Marinus of Tyre of whom I have already spoken. Marinus collected information from mariners and travellers and he set out to correct the errors of his predecessors, but he died prematurely and his work no longer exists. The geography of Ptolemy was written half a century after the work of Marinus and was what we may call a new and revised edition of Marinus. The invention of printing and engraving in the fifteenth century no doubt had much to do with the revival of the work of Ptolemy in the fifteenth century and of map production generally. Apart from the invention of printing and its stimulating effect, Portuguese, Greek and French cartographers appear as competitors with the Italian, Catalonian and Balearic artists. The oldest manuscript of Ptolemy known to be in existence was made about 1200 and this was issued in facsimile in Paris in 1867. The earliest printed edition (1475) was issued without maps. A very early metrical version by Berlinghieri exists and is noteworthy as being the first book with maps wholly engraved. The Ptolemy of 1508 is as I have said, remarkable as containing the Ruysch map which is the first printed map showing any part of America with the exception of the Waldseemüller map of 1507 (reproduced in 1901). The Waldseemüller map is the oldest map with the name America on it. The Ruysch map does not give the name. The map of Ruysch, however, marks an epoch in the development of maps.

* Beazley, I., 379. † A list of editions of Ptolemy is given in Phillips, I., 105-6. ‡ Andrews.

In addition to its great interest to Americans, it is (1) the first printed map of the world on which the discoveries of the Portuguese along the coasts of Africa are laid down; (2) the first map in print on which India is drawn as a triangular peninsula projecting from the south coast of Asia; (3) the first printed map on which the interior and eastern parts of Asia are no longer delineated exclusively from material collected by Marinus of Tyre and Ptolemy. There are other important features found in the Ruysch map which Nordenskiöld has pointed out in his *Facsimile Atlas*, pp. 63-67. Those who wish to make a special study of this map by Ruysch should get Thacher's *Continent of America* (1896) in which the legends as well as the nomenclature of the map are fully dealt with.

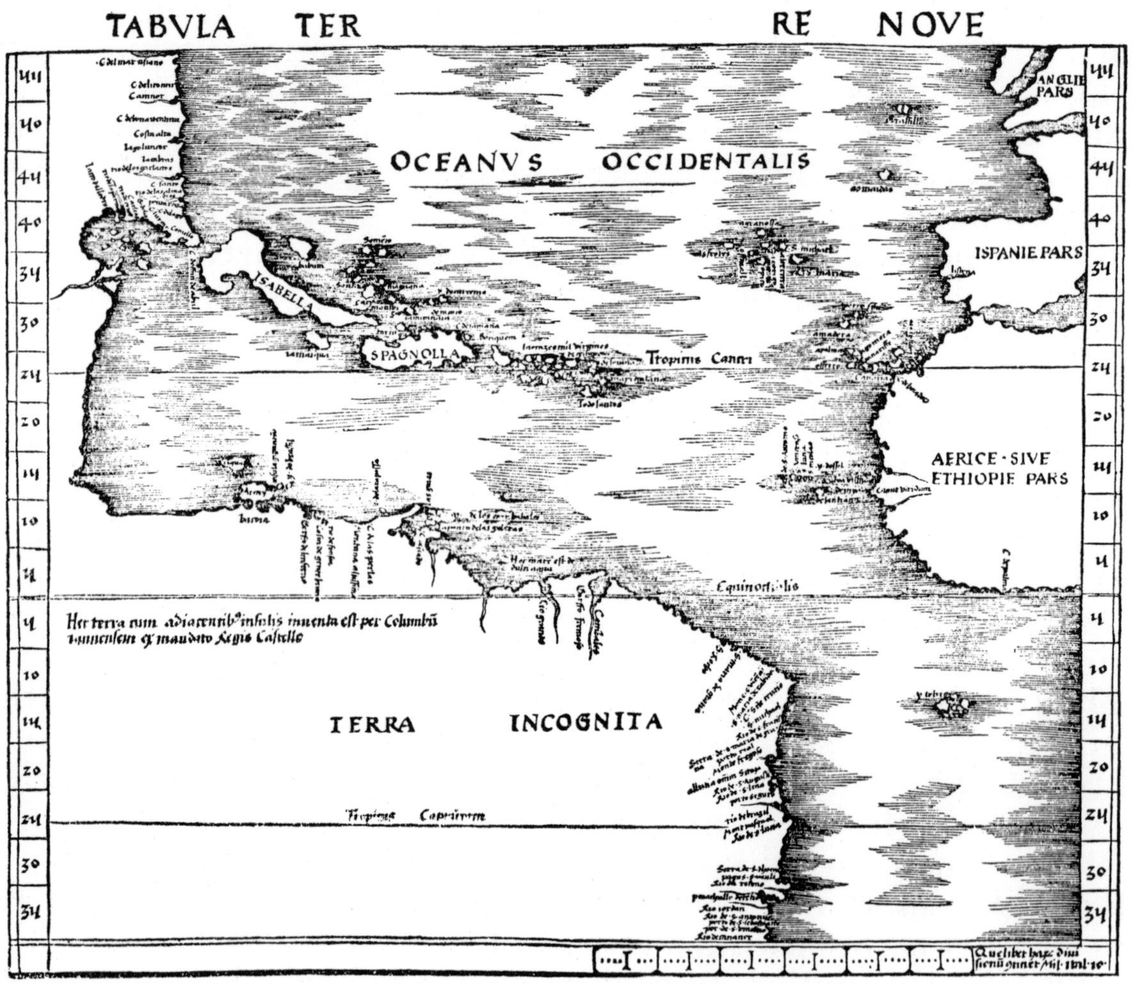

TABULA OCEANI OCCIDENTALIS SIVE TERRÆ NOVÆ. From the 1513 edition of Ptolemy.

Ptolemy's maps represent the Greek idea of the world. There is a vast gulf between them and the far more exact and intelligently made Portolans of the Italians and Catalans. In an inspired passage Mr. Beazley, when speaking of the legacy of maps from the ancient world and specially of Ptolemy's maps, says of them "Whatever their merits, minute knowledge of coast lines and serviceable accuracy in delineation are not among them. We must look elsewhere for material which could readily assist the practical mariner and in the history of human knowledge there are few stranger chapters than that which records the influence of the Ptolemaic revival in delaying the formation of an accurate world map in the fifteenth, sixteenth and seventeenth centuries."*

In the early sixteenth century the study of the sciences was interesting men of culture and opportunities were afforded of correcting Ptolemy's maps. Maps of the world were put forth by Peter Apianus, Oronce Finé, Sebastian Cabot and others. Then came a great landmark in map production—Mercator's world map of 1569. It was Mercator's intention to produce a complete collection of new maps, but he died in 1594 and the publication of this first atlas (1595) was left to his son, who issued the book a few months after his father's death. So renowned a map maker as was Mercator and so great a pioneer deserves some special tribute here.

Gerard Mercator was born on March 5, 1512, in a small town called Rupelmonde in East Flanders, about eight miles from Antwerp. He was the son of a shoemaker and the youngest of six children. The name Mercator is a Latinisation of his original name which was De Cremer, the name Cremer being the equivalent of the German Kremer or Krämer, and meaning tradesman or shopkeeper. Mercator's parents died when he was thirteen or fourteen years of age and he had to rely upon a great uncle for help. This assistance readily came and Mercator was enabled to study at the school or college of Bois-le-Duc in Brabant and afterwards at the University of Louvain. When faced with the problem of earning his own livelihood he chose for his occupation the manufacture of mathematical instruments and added to this as "side shows" the drawing, engraving and illuminating or colouring of maps and charts. He established a workshop of his own, and here he manufactured astrolabes, globes and instruments of such scientific accuracy and superior workmanship that the products of his skill found a ready market.†

Mercator began his career as a map maker by executing a map of Palestine. Religious movements just then caused maps

* Beazley, III., 517. † Elial Hall, *Mercator*, p. 166.

of the Holy Land to be in demand. His next map was one of Flanders undertaken at the suggestion of some Flemish merchants. For the execution of this map Mercator travelled all over the country, taking three years to complete the survey. Both these maps were published at Louvain, but no copy of either is in existence. In 1554 Mercator published a large map of Europe but of this no copy can be traced. In 1564 he executed a map of Great Britain which had been sent to him to be engraved by a friend in England. A few years later Mercator put forth the chart which made him famous and which has transmitted his name and made it familiar for three hundred and fifty years. The significance of Mercator's chart upon his projection is that in it he says to the mariner—"if you wish to sail from one port to another here is a chart and a straight line on it, and if you follow carefully this line you will certainly arrive at your port of destination. But the length of the line may not be correct and I warn you that although its length may not be correct yet it points in the right direction. Consequently if you adhere to the line you may get to your destination sooner or you may not get there as soon as you expect, but you will certainly get there."*

As far as it is known, only a single copy of the original issue of Mercator's chart is now in existence. It is preserved in the Bibliothèque Nationale in Paris, and it is facsimiled in Jomard's *Monuments de Géographie.*

Mercator's chart stands alone in map history, isolated from the many other works he accomplished. It was not heralded by any previous announcement and no mention appears to have been made of it in his subsequent publications. He was a prophet without honour in his own time. Even after his death his successors did not think "the projection" of sufficient account to give it a place in the Atlas. We know, however, that early in the seventeenth century the French seaport of Dieppe was the principal depôt for the publication and the sale of nautical charts and that those then sold at Dieppe were on Mercator's projection. Modern geography and map making really date from Mercator. Although Mercator was a student of Ptolemy he shewed much independence in not following him too closely. Ptolemy's geography had stood as the highest authority for more than twelve hundred years and even in the lifetime of Mercator Ptolemy provided the groundwork of geographical study. In 1578 Mercator produced a revised edition of Ptolemy with maps

* Elial Hall, p. 180.

engraved on copper, and in 1584 he issued another edition. These two editions of Ptolemy added greatly to Mercator's reputation, but he was not content to stop there and for the next ten years (he died in December, 1594) he devoted his energies to producing the first collection of maps which bore the name "Atlas." There is every reason to believe that Mercator in issuing this first atlas had projected a vast encyclopædia of the Sciences of which his volume, merely called "Atlas" and not "The Atlas" or "An Atlas," was to be the first volume. It was issued posthumously in the year 1595 by Rumold Mercator, the geographer's son, a few months after his father's death. The maps making up this now very rare atlas had appeared in three numbers in 1585, 1590 and 1595. A year or so later and after the date of Mercator's death the engraved copper plates of all the Mercator maps and charts fell by purchase into the possession of Jodocus Hondius of Amsterdam, who in 1606 brought out a new edition to which he added fifty new maps, including a few American ones. Thus began what is known as the Hondius-Mercator Atlas. The text was furnished by Montanus and the new maps were engraved by Petrus Kaerius. Kaerius also prepared for Hondius the maps for the *Atlas minor* issued the following year (1607). Many editions in various languages followed. Over a period of seventy-five years Hondius and his successors at Amsterdam published fifty editions of the Mercator Atlas. In the 1607 edition there appears the first general map of America which gives to North and South America their respective names. The fourth edition (1613) contains portraits of Mercator and the elder Hondius, and there were ten American maps in this edition.

In 1635 the English text appeared with the following title: *Historia Mundi; or, Mercator's Atlas.....Lately rectified in divers places, and also beautiful and enlarged with new mappes and tables by the studious industry of Iudocus Hondy. Englished by W.S., London;* and of this there was a second edition in 1637.

The English market was also supplied with another English version, published much more sumptuously, in two large folios, at Amsterdam in 1636, with the title, *Atlas; or, a Geographical Description of the Regions...of the World, represented by New and Exact Maps. Translated by Henry Hexham. Printed at Amsterdam by Henry Hondius and John Johnstone.* The American maps are in the second volume, where the map of the two Americas is much like the world-map in vol. i.

A still further enlargement of the Mercator-Hondius *Atlas novus* took place in 1638, when it appeared in three imperial folio volumes, with 318 maps, 17 of which are special maps of America. It was now more commonly known as Jannson's Atlas, and it went on increasing till it grew to eight volumes, to which were added a volume, *Orbis Maritimus* (1657), a second on the ancient world, a celestial atlas for a third, and an *Atlas Contractus,* or *resumé,* for the fourth; making twelve in all.*

A contemporary of Mercator and a friendly rival was Abraham Ortelius. A lifelong friendship existed between these two great pioneers and no conflict of interest or jealousy was ever allowed to disturb it. Both men were natives of the same bit of country, both having been born on the banks of the Scheldt. They travelled together, making a tour of France in company with one another. Ortelius was a man of education and great knowledge, but he had no practical acquaintance with map making and engraving. Next to Mercator, Ortelius stands as the greatest geographer of his age and period. His real name was Abraham Ortel, but he fell a victim to the fashion of using a Latinised name and he has come down to posterity as Ortelius and so he will continue. Although Ortelius was of German parentage (as indeed was Mercator) he was born at Antwerp in 1527 and he died there in 1598. Travelling was his passion as suited his profession. He visited the Netherlands and Germany in 1575, England and Ireland in 1577, and Italy on several occasions. He was one of the first collectors of maps and his

* The following is a list of the various editions of Mercator's *Atlas Major:*

Latin text ... ... pt. 1.	1585
,, ,, ... ,, 2.	1590
,, ,, ... ,, 3.	1595
PUBLISHED AS A WHOLE:	
1st. Latin ed.	1602
2nd. ,, ,, ...	1606
3rd. ,, ,, ...	1607
(*2nd of Hondius*)	
4th. ,, ,, ...	1608
(*A reprint of 1607*)	
1st. French ed.	1609
5th. Latin ed.	1611
6th. ,, ,, ...	1613
2nd. French ed.	1613
7th. Latin ed.	1616
3rd. French ed.	1619
8th. Latin ed.	1619
9th. ,, ,, ...	1623
(*Called by error 5th ed.*)	
10th. Latin ed.	1627
11th. Latin ed.	1628
4th. French ed.	1628
12th. Latin ed.	1630
5th. French ed.	1630
(*Last four editions all have same title-page and are by error all called the 10th.*)	
13th. Latin ed.	1631
(*Also has same title as 1628, 1630*)	
1st. German ed., 2v.	1633
6th. French ed., 2v.	1633
? Latin ed.	1633
1st. Dutch ed.	1634
7th. French ed., 2v.	1635
1st. English ed. (*Historia Mundi*)	1635
2nd. English ed. (same) ...	1637
English ed. (Hexham) ...	1636
14th. Latin ed., 3v.	1638
2nd. Dutch ed., 3v.	1638
2nd. German ed.	1638

Theatrum Orbis Terrarum issued in 1570 was the first modern Atlas, although, as we have seen, it was reserved for Mercator to be the first to use the word "Atlas."

Most of the maps in Ortelius's *Theatrum* (1570) were admittedly reproductions of the maps by various geographers, but this first collected series of maps is a noble volume, a monument of rare erudition and industry. The story of its initiation is worth telling. An Antwerp merchant named Hooftman had begun in the sixteenth century to collect old maps. His nautical curiosity developed and his collection increased. He soon found that the job of rolling up and unrolling his large maps was a nuisance, so Abraham Ortelius was commissioned to obtain as many single sheet maps as he could find and to stitch and bind them in a volume. Having in this way put together about thirty maps for his master Hooftman, Ortelius decided to extend the benefits to all scholars and to publish a book of maps. Thus began the Atlas by which Ortelius is known to all geographers. The first edition of this great work, which stands as yet another landmark in the history of maps, was issued at Antwerp on May 20th, 1570. A second edition appeared in the same year, followed by many others until 1612.*

A feature of interest in many editions of Ortelius's Atlas is the list he gives of contemporary cartographers, etc. This list

* Chronological list of the folio editions of the *Theatrum*, as found in Hessel's *Abrahami Ortelii Epistvlæ*:—

1570. Latin. Dated xx maji. (*Verso of t.p. blank*)
1570. Latin (3 impressions, not dated as above)
1571. Latin.
1571. Dutch.
1572. German.
1573. Additamentum (*perhaps also with Dutch and German text*)
1573. Latin.
1573. German.
1574. Latin.
1575. Latin.
1578. French.
1579. Latin.
1580. Additamentum II.
1580. German.
1581. French.
1584. Additamentum III.
1584. Latin.
1585. Additamentum III. (*With French text.*)
1587. French.
1588. Spanish.
1589. Latin.
1590. Additamentum IV. (*Also in German.*)
1591. Latin.
1592. Latin.
1595. Additamentum V.
1595. Latin.
1598. Dutch.
1598. French.
1601. Latin.
1602. Spanish.
1602. German.
1603. Latin.
1606. English.
1607. Latin.
1608. Italian.
1609. Latin.
1612. Latin.
1612. Italian.
1612. Spanish.
1624. Parergon.

has been reprinted with many additional notes by Nordenskiöld in his *Facsimile Atlas*. It may be compared with the even more valuable "Biographical notes concerning Portuguese and Spanish Pilot majors, pilots and cartographers of the first half of the sixteenth century," to be found in Henry Harrisse's *The Discovery of North America* (London, 1892.) On the engraved title of Ortelius's *Theatrum* there are four female figures representing the four divisions of the world, and thus in this book America is for the first time admitted into the realm of symbolism as the equal of the other parts of the Globe. A complete study of the peculiarities in these early maps collected by Ortelius would reveal much curious map lore. For instance Ortelius in his map of Gloucestershire shews Teuxberi (Tewkesbury) but not Gloucester. Uphill, a small village in Somerset, is given as of equal importance with Bristol. Wiltshire and Wight (Isle of Wight) are both spelt in the Sam Weller fashion with a V.

Before Mercator or Ortelius had issued their atlases, there appeared, independently of the many editions of Ptolemy, collections of single maps of various countries. The Germans and the Swiss were busily engaged in producing maps, and the Italians, the Spaniards and the Portuguese held a high place. Although a new era in cartography must for ever be dated from Ortelius and Mercator who, as we have seen, did such fine work during the latter half of the sixteenth century, injustice is often done to map draughtsmen of the earlier decades of the same century, and the cause for this neglect is found in the fact that these earlier maps were issued as single sheets and were rarely, if ever, bound up in volumes. They were therefore easily destroyed and few have been preserved. This more especially applies to the maps issued in Rome about the middle of the sixteenth century under the name of Lafreri, a collection of whose maps is now of the greatest rarity.

As will be seen from Mr. Henry Stevens's Catalogue appended to this volume, the Macpherson Collection includes numerous publications of extreme rarity, an item of exceptional interest in this respect being the *Isolario* of Bartolommeo dalli Sonnetti, which is believed to be not only the earliest atlas of the Mediterranean but also possibly the earliest printed atlas of any kind.

So far, the maps we have dealt with have not in all cases been decorative. A well coloured copy of Ptolemy or Ortelius may, however, prove highly attractive and in the early Portolan charts there are attempts and successful ones, too, at heraldic decoration. I have said how the Papal banner is seen in some flying over Avignon, while certain towns are marked by groups of turrets. The early *mappæmondi,* too, are always pictorial maps though not so attractive in a way. They deal with legendary and mythical geography of the middle ages and include pictures of monstrosities, etc., in human form, which were supposed to tenant the unknown regions of the earth. After Marco Polo and Columbus had brought about a revolution in the knowledge of the world, old symbolism gradually made way for new forms of ornament, and the ship, the fisherman, the mermaid and the sea-horse were in use as ornament on the maps found in the first atlases. Furthermore, map colouring became an art, and although crude at first soon developed, as I shall point out, into something highly decorative and ornamental with much more delicacy and refinement in the putting on of the colours. After the publication of the atlases by Ortelius (1570) and Mercator (1595), the centre of map production was transferred to Holland and almost entirely to Amsterdam. Here it was that Jodocus Hondius (1563-1611), the brother-in-law of the younger Mercator and his son Henry Hondius were found worthy successors to carry on the great geographical work of mapping out the world. Hondius had his establishment at the sign of "The Watch Dog," which appeared on his books as follows :—*Amstelodami ex officina Judoci Hondii sub signo Canis Vigilio, anno 1616.* Hondius is the Latinised form of Hondt (a dog) and the shop sign of the watch dog was a pun on the proprietor's name. For a time the elder Hondius was resident in London, where he had set up as a typefounder and an engraver of maps and charts and assisted John Speed with his atlas. When Jodocus Hondius died in 1611, the publication of his atlases was continued by his son Hendrick and his son-in-law Jan Jansson, a member of a family who played a very prominent part in the history and development of Dutch maps. By the year 1630 the Mercator atlas as issued by the Hondius firm had included in it at least a dozen maps more or less associated with America. In the 1633 edition there were thirty-three maps bearing directly or indirectly upon America.

It was fortunate for the history of maps that the Dutch in the early years of the seventeenth century made them their special study and cartography at Amsterdam developed into a great and profitable industry. It was an industry, too, which fitted in with many other lucrative trades they carried on in valuable commodities. The fact that the Dutch had already captured the carrying trade of the world brought a vast amount of geographical knowledge to their doors at first hand by men who sailed the seas. The sciences most nearly associated with geography were studied and high ideals of business and scholarship ran side by side. The men of the Netherlands in the seventeenth century grew up not only great merchants, but like the Elzevirs, they united with commerce great scholarship. Several of Vermeer's pictures reveal the dominating interest in map production which pervaded Holland at the time he was painting.

Willem Janszoon Blaeu, the most distinguished Dutch map and globe maker, was one of the most notable map workers in the history of cartography. He was born at the village of Alkmaar in 1571, but of his early years and parentage little or nothing is known. He gravitated to Amsterdam and first found employment as a joiner's apprentice. Soon after this we hear of him living on the Danish island of Hveen in close friendship with Tycho Brahe, the famous astronomer, who had here established his great observatory which soon became one of the most famous centres in Europe for study. After two years with him—years that laid the foundation of his scientific knowledge—Blaeu returned to Amsterdam about 1597 and started as a maker of mathematical instruments and of maps and globes as well as an engraver and printer.

Blaeu surveyed all that had already been done in the way of map making and map collecting by Mercator and Ortelius and he decided that he would found a geographical establishment in which the arts of engraving, printing and designing should have free scope. Over the door of his original establishment a gilded sundial as a trade sign was fixed on the globe. Here he carried on his business until 1637, when he moved into larger premises in the Blumengracht. He died in the year 1638 and the business passed into the hands of his sons John and Cornelius Blaeu. In 1672 the entire establishment was burned down and many fine atlases were destroyed. The younger generation of Blaeus were worthy successors of the father, and the following account of the Blaeu establishment while under the direction of the two sons gives interesting sidelights upon the extensive operations of the great Atlas firm.

"'On the Blumengracht,' says Filips von Zesen, in his description of the city of Amsterdam, 'near the third bridge, and the third alley, may be found the greatly renowned printing house of John Blaeu, Counsellor and Magistrate, of the city. It is furnished with nine type presses, named after the nine Muses, six presses for copperplate printing, and a type foundry. The entire establishment on the canal, with the adjoining house in which the proprietor lives, is 75 feet in breadth, and stretches along the east side of a cross street 135 feet, or with the attached house 150 feet. Fronting on the canal is a room with cases in which the copper plates are kept, from which the Atlases, the Book of the Cities of the Netherlands and of foreign countries, also the Mariner's Atlases and other choice books are printed, and which must have cost a ton of gold. Next to this first room is a press room used for plate printing, and opening upon the cross street referred to above is a place where the type, from which impressions have been made, was washed; then follows in order the room for book printing, which resembles a long hall with numerous windows on either side. In the extreme rear is a room in which the type and certain other materials used in printing are stored. Opposite this store room is a stairway leading to a small room above which is set apart for the use of the proof-readers, where first and second impressions are carefully looked over, and the errors corrected which have been made by the typesetters. In front of this last designated room is a long table or bench on which the final prints are placed as soon as they are brought from the press, and where they are left for a considerable time. In the story above is a table for the same purpose just indicated, at the extreme end of which, and over the room occupied by the proof-readers, is the type foundry wherein the letters used in the printing of the various languages are moulded.' ''*

In the introduction to the Blaeu Atlas of 1635 there is a touching paragraph in which one of the younger Blaeus speaks with filial admiration of his father's work and states how he (the elder Blaeu) started to make maps because being stimulated by the examples of the great geographers he decided to devote his life to mapping out the world. It may be noted as a proof of the confidence his contemporaries had in his knowledge of geography and the science of navigation that the States General of Amsterdam in 1633 by resolution appointed Blaeu map maker to the Republic, a position held by him until his death when the honour was passed on to his son and to his grandson. In a further resolution of October 23rd, 1666, we read that no house engaged in commerce will be allowed to send any marine maps to India or to have them taken by captains of vessels except those made at the Blaeu establishment. Blaeu's great printing establishment was one of the wonders of the time and brought him great fame. The map engravers employed by him were the most skilled in the Netherlands, his types were beautiful and artistic and possessed simplicity and dignity. When he borrowed maps from other publishers—and there was a lot of borrowing from one another in

* E. L. Stevenson, *W. J. Blaeu*, pp. 17-18.

those days—he always greatly improved them by his own re-engraving and all his maps reveal superior excellence in line, letter and ornamentation.*

Blaeu's first atlas of land maps appeared in 1631 and it was what it professed in its title to be, a supplement to Mercator and Ortelius. It was entitled *Appendix Theatri Ortelii et Atlantis Mercatoris.* It gathered together many maps already issued singly by Blaeu himself and other map makers. It contains one hundred and three maps with text usually printed on the back of the map. In letters to a friend written about this time Blaeu states that it is his constant endeavour to improve his maps. In 1634 he writes to the same friend : "It is my intention to place two or three provinces on one sheet, but it will be necessary, however, to leave some open space in which I can write the titles of the maps, arms of the country and the scale of miles." Later, he again writes : "I shall give special attention to the engraving of the plates, printing lightly from them at first in order that changes may be made before the final engraving is done." It is clear from these extracts from Blaeu's letters to his friend Schickard that the perfecting of his maps occupied Blaeu's day and night thoughts. After the publication of his first two or three minor atlases he decided to start on what is known as the *Atlas Major*. It was completed and issued after William Blaeu's death, however, appearing in 1662 in eleven volumes. A second edition of the first volume appeared in 1665, all the other volumes of the set bearing the date 1662. In 1663 a French edition in twelve volumes was published, and a second edition of this translation appeared in 1667. The French edition resembles the original edition of 1662 which had its text in Latin, except in the extension of the letterpress with regard to some countries, the narrative part dealing with France and Switzerland, and being enlarged to fill two volumes instead of one. A Spanish translation also appeared, but this was nearly all destroyed in Blaeu's great fire in 1672. The Spanish edition is therefore now very rare. Although fairly large editions were issued in each language, the *Atlas Major* is now difficult to procure in any of its translated forms. The number of volumes varies with the language in which the edition is printed. The number and the quality of the maps do not differ much. Copies were printed on Dutch paper of remarkably fine quality which has kept its clean and spotless whiteness to this day. Special copies of the *Atlas Major*

* E. L. Stevenson, p. 40.

were prepared for people of great renown. Admiral de Ruyter is said to have had a fine copy bound for him, and a copy bound in purple was presented to the Sultan of Blaeu's day, which pleased him so much that he ordered its translation into the Turkish language. Of the eleven volumes of the *Atlas Major,* Volume Five deals with England, containing a set of magnificent county maps; Volume Six deals with Scotland, Volume Seven is devoted to France, Volume Eight to Italy, Volume Ten to Asia and Volume Eleven to North and South America. A complete list of the maps in each volume is given in Phillip's list, Volume III, pp. 146-164. A list of the various atlases issued by Blaeu is found in Tiele's *Nederlandsche Bibliographie,* 1884, and in Phillip's List, Volume I, pp. 196-7.

Blaeu brought under contribution to his atlases any competent enthusiast he could attach. In the case of the maps of Scotland which appear in Blaeu's *Atlas Major,* these were done by Timothy Pont, who as early as 1600 had been appointed minister to the Scotch parish of Dunnett in remote Caithness. Pont's ministerial duties could not have been very heavy and he appears to have found his pastoral work consistent with long absences from his parish. No one has yet explained how with the country undrained, unfenced and almost without roads as Scotland then was, Pont managed to achieve what he did. Pont did not live to see his maps produced by Blaeu on magnificent paper and with heraldic borders and ornaments. At Pont's death about 1612, his maps of Scotland were purchased by Sir John Scot of Scotstarvet. At the request of King Charles I. these maps were completed by Sir Robert Gordon of Straloch, and in 1645 they were taken to Amsterdam by Sir John Scot who superintended their publication for Blaeu's atlas.

Not enough has yet been said of Blaeu's influence with regard to map decoration. Before Blaeu came on the scene, map printing and ornamentation were in a very crude state. No praise could be too high for the work Blaeu accomplished in applying not only his great geographical and scientific knowledge to the planning of his maps but also his sense of beauty and of ornament. In many branches of art the Dutch have reached the highest pinnacles and everyone knows that as a nation they would never tolerate bad art. Blaeu's maps were put forth both plain and coloured. Collectors will not require to be told that the maps coloured by the clever hands of contemporary colourists in Blaeu's office are much more desirable possessions than the plain copies. It may be as well to point out that all who are buying Blaeu's maps should try to secure copies with contemporary colouring. The separate maps offered frequently by dealers are in most cases maps detached from the big atlases. In many cases they are copies which have been coloured by map artists of to-day. When complete atlases cannot be secured—and they are now very scarce—it is always worth while to secure odd volumes. Those who look at a coloured map of the sixteenth or the seventeenth century and then at plain uncoloured ones will see at once to what a fine art map colouring attained in Holland in Blaeu's day. We know little or nothing of the names of the colourists nor do we know the names of the designers of the noble cartouches which as ornament were applied to Dutch maps. Timothy Pont would certainly have been a little surprised to have seen one of his maps after it had passed through Blaeu's establishment, where there were added to it picturesque figures of natives wearing wide brimmed bonnets or others dressed up in kilt, plaid and hose. The map of Aberdeen in Blaeu's big Atlas shews a fine kilted figure and the map of Lorn one with a feathered glengarry. In the French maps a country gentleman is depicted with an attendant out hawking, equipped with hoods, lures, gloves, hunting sword and bugle. On another is a church, past which marches a body of soldiers followed by women carrying provisions on their heads and all drawn with skill and vigour.* As we turn over the pages of Blaeu's *Atlas Major* we are fascinated by the groups of comely men and women or of chubby Dutch babies. Here are plans, too, of Dutch cities which are full and minute and which illustrate many local and domestic customs. The garden is depicted laid out to the smallest flower, or again we see a group of men playing bowls or refreshing themselves in a little pleasure house. The title pages, too, are masterpieces, and in one instance Blaeu has done touching honour to his first great master, Tycho Brahe, by depicting him and his assistant in his great observatory. The astronomer is seated calm, majestic and superbly dressed, while his assistants all round are busily making observations with various instruments. It is, however, in the small details of ornament that Blaeu's maps excel and rank higher than any others. He adopts the old traditional ornaments on maps, the whale, the ship and the seahorse, but he draws as well upon a wide range of other subjects. Even in the smaller atlas of 1642-55 issued in six volumes, there are illustrations of five

* Sir H. Maxwell, *Blaeu's Atlas.*

hundred ships, two hundred costume pictures and one thousand coats-of-arms or village scenes. The miscellaneous ornament includes neptunes, tritons, dolphins, river gods, the flatness of the sea is relieved by sea monsters, flying fish, mermaids and unicorns. The well drawn instruments include astrolabes, globes and compasses. There are galleons, there are fishermen and there are charming flags. There are stags and wild boars and all kinds of indigenous as well as mythical animals. There are lovely allegorical figures and festoons and scroll work, cupids, cornucopiæ, agricultural implements, reapers and cornstacks —all in most attractive settings and coloured in most gay and harmonious colourings. No one has, as far as I am aware, made a descriptive list of all the geographical books in addition to great atlases issued by the Blaeu firm. No such list would be satisfactory unless it emphasised the beauty of such a volume as the work on Brazil by Caspar Barlaeus, which contains in its finest form about twenty-five coloured maps and twenty-nine coloured views, including ships, natives, settlers in costume and coast-line pictures. The fine and full output of the firm of Blaeu is one of the most remarkable in the whole history of seventeenth century publishing, a period when the book had become commercialised and had lost much of its beauty as regards paper and illustrations and such details as title pages. It was the pride of the Blaeus to rescue the book from those who had little or no taste and who were merely commercial in their ends and aims. The Blaeu family were princely fellows in all they did. Just as Ortelius had been "Geographer to Philip II. of Spain," so Blaeu became appropriately "Map maker to the Republic of the Netherlands."

It could hardly be expected that the Blaeus would meet with no rivalry. The elder Blaeu had early in life found a competitor in Jansson. Jansson was a brother-in-law of Hondius and was associated with him in business. When Hondius died in 1638 Jansson continued the business of map publishing. The three daughters of Jan Jansson married three sons of Jean von Waesberg. All these three sons took the names of Jansson and two of them allied themselves with Jan Jansson and conducted their business under the name Janssonius. Jansson produced in 1633 a rival to the earliest Blaeu atlas. It had one hundred and six maps. In 1638 it was called *Atlas Novus* which had seventeen maps of America. In 1639 a French edition was called *Nouveau Theatre du monde,* with new maps by Henry Hondius, son of

Jodocus Hondius. Eighteen of these maps were American, including New England and Virginia. A fifth part of the *Nouveau Theatre* was added in 1657 containing coast charts of America. In 1652-3 Jansson issued a five volume atlas which besides about twenty maps relating to America had a whole volume with fifty-six maps devoted to the British Isles. Jansson reached his best about the year 1661, when his *Orbis Antiquus* was published. For the collector one of the finest specimens of Jansson's work is the *Illustriorum Hispaniæ Urbium Tabulæ*. This is a collection of views and plans of Spanish towns, the greater number of which were executed by George Hoefnagle. The book with its coloured designs is highly attractive and decorative. Jansson, although so enterprising, can never supersede Blaeu because his presses were not as good and his paper was inferior. He makes, however, a good second to Blaeu and collectors should endeavour to secure at any rate one book of Jansson and for preference the one I name upon Spanish towns. Jansson achieved a remarkable record, for working with materials left him by his father-in-law, Jodocus Hondius, he produced a fine Dutch Atlas in six volumes, a French in six volumes, a German in nine and a Latin in two.

Jansson was not the first map publisher to put forth views and plans of towns as apart from his maps. In 1572-1618 George Braun and Francis Hogenberg published a work of extreme beauty and charm entitled *Civitates Orbis Terrarum*. The title of Ortelius's Collection of maps was *Theatrum Orbis Terrarum* and Ortelius always regarded Braun and Hogenberg's book as a companion work to his own—the one dealing with countries and the other with towns. The book has come down to us as Braun and Hogenberg's book, but there was another enterprising man associated with the work, and this was George Hoefnagle. Hoefnagle's name frequently turns up in map history in the sixteenth and seventeenth centuries and it is always attached to some view or map of beauty. Hoefnagle united with his topographical art the business of a dealer in jewels, but when Antwerp was plundered by the Spaniards and he and his father lost everything they took refuge in Bavaria where he found scope to exercise his talents. He was an engraver as well as an artist and he had been employed by Ortelius to do some of the maps for his *Theatrum*. He had indeed travelled with Ortelius as his friend and collaborator. Braun speaks of Hoefnagle as "a most illustrious man." Hoefnagle's name will continue a notable one among map designers and specially will he be remembered as the artist associated with Braun and Hogenberg's book. This fine book is not often found complete, but it should at all times be bought when in a clean condition. Occasionally it is found coloured by a contemporary colourist's hand, and no map book is more to be desired than a coloured copy of Braun and Hogenberg. The title pages, the costume figures in the foreground, the red roofs of the houses and the arms of the towns when done in colour make a most charming work to possess. In the plan or view of Bristol, for instance, the costume of the figures fits the period of the map —the peculiar circular buckler used in the sixteenth century being prominent in the hands of a soldier. The book was begun originally at Cologne in 1572 and not completed till 1618. It contains about three hundred and fifty illustrations and in a large number of instances they are the earliest pictorial representations of the places included. A considerable number of views of English towns and cities are embraced. London, Chester, Bristol, Edinburgh, Canterbury and Exeter being among them, while there are as well a number of small views of York, Shrewsbury and other old English towns. A complete list of places included in Braun's book may be found in Phillips, III, pp. 17-25. On similar lines to Braun and Hogenberg's book is Deventer's *Atlas des villes de Belgique au XVI siècle* and a later work by P. van der Aa, *La Galerie Agréable du Monde,* containing three thousand plates and maps by the best Dutch engravers, the plates for which had been obtained largely from Blaeu, Visscher, De Wit and others. As regards London maps, plans and views, the names of those chiefly concerned in their making were Ralph Agas, a land surveyor and a native of Stoke by Nayland. In November, 1606, he is in Holborn, at the end of Fetter Lane, "near the sign of the Helmet." John Norden, probably from Wiltshire and an M.A. of Oxford, who devoted his life to mapping out the home counties, Wenceslaus Hollar, a famous native of Prague, whose numerous views date from 1647, and William Faithorne, a Londoner, settled near Temple Bar and found afterwards at Blackfriars—these are but one or two of those whose plans and views are of great value and interest to the collector. The London Topographical Society has reproduced much early London cartographic work. There is also Ogilby and Morgan's great map of London and Westminster (about 1682) in which, besides much that is pictorial and decorative, there is given the frontage of individual houses in the principal streets and squares.

Confusion often arises regarding sixteenth and seventeenth century maps because so many of them have been very inaccurately or vaguely described, being sometimes known by the name of the publisher, sometimes the engraver, and sometimes the originator or surveyor. In describing a sixteenth century view such as is found in Braun and Hogenberg's book, or a seventeenth century map such as may be seen in one of the Mercator-Hondius atlases, we ought to seek wherever possible for information under the following headings: (1) originator, author or surveyor; (2) engraver or reproducer; (3) employment of symbols; (4) ornamentation, including border lines and framings; (5) date; (6) heraldry; (7) any notes as to alteration of old plates. All who collect old maps should note these particulars with regard to each map in their possession and add to each as much information as can be discovered regarding publishers, sellers, engravers, watermarks, dimensions and colouring, as to whether contemporary or more recent.*

As soon as map-making became a wide-spread industry the publication of local maps was increasingly popular. Zeal for topography had an outlet in the drawing of maps of special areas and thus it was that there came into being the first county maps.

In 1563, Laurence Nowell, a member of a family distinguished in the Church and himself Dean of Lichfield a few years later, wrote a letter to Sir William Cecil saying that it was his intention to make maps of all the English counties. The results of his exemplary efforts may be found in the British Museum (Cottonian MSS. Domitian XVIII, fol. 97-123). Nowell's maps are drawn with peculiar neatness, but on too small a scale to be of practical use. Nowell being an Anglo-Saxon scholar, the names of all places are expressed in Saxon characters. The letter which follows shews that the craft of map making had not up to the date of this letter (1563) emerged from the superstitions of the dark ages. As Saxton's Atlas did not appear before 1579 Nowell must be regarded as a pioneer in the making of maps of the English counties.

Laurence Nowell to Sir William Cecil, complaining of the inaccuracy of the general Maps of England, and stating his design of constructing Maps of all the Counties, if he should meet with Sir William's encouragement. A.D. 1563.

I am aware, right honourable Sir, that you take the greatest interest in all monuments of the liberal arts, and especially in maps, since you

* Dr. William Martin.

know how to reap the benefit from them which enables you both to perform more fitly the duties pertaining to your office and to be incessant in your efforts in every way to benefit the State. Furthermore, I have observed that those who have hitherto undertaken the task of describing England have never yet given you satisfaction, and that they have never (for I will speak as I feel) produced anything that deserves even moderate commendation. Nor is this to be wondered at, since, without any fixed rules, without the aid of art and judgement,* either relying upon the reports of others, or trusting to the uncertain conjectural inferences of their eyes, they have filled their maps with imaginary sites and intervals. Wherefore, since I felt confident that I myself could render some service in a work of such a kind, and at the same time often thought how ill-suited I was for most other duties, I had long had in mind to offer my help and steady application in this matter, so that I might both be to some extent useful to my country and the State and might also show my gratitude to you to whom I owe so much. I have hitherto been prevented from doing this out of consideration for those who have been so long engaged in the same task; for I was afraid that, if I laid hands upon the harvest of others, I might be suspected by you of a sort of unlawful ambition. But above all the thought of your censure deterred me, for I greatly feared that I might seem either to decline or neglect the task which you had imposed upon me. However, seeing that as yet they have produced nothing worthy of what has been so long and so anxiously expected, and since I can readily understand that my assistance will not long continue necessary to the Earl of Oxford, trusting in your accustomed goodness and kindness to me, I have not hesitated to inform you of this my intention. I await your authority and judgement in the matter; for I am quite ready to do this or anything else you command, to the best of my ability. But, if I may express myself frankly, there is no public task, as far as I know, which I feel confident I can perform more satisfactorily than this, or which I should more willingly desire to undertake and carry out. I certainly hope, if only the light of your benevolence shine upon me in this matter, to portray not only the whole of our country but every part of it and each of the counties, so that in the future there will no need of spending more labour or money upon the matter. Further, unless my hope deceives me, no unworthy monument, dedicated to you, will remain in the royal archives, one that will endure and will be of great service to your posterity, as long as the English empire and State shall last. Farewell.

Your most devoted servant,

LAURENCE NOWELL.

To the right honorable and his singular
good maister Sir Willm Cecill, Knight,
the Quens Ma[ties] principall Secretarie.

* This might perhaps also be translated: "without the aid and judgment of art," but the above version seems more probable.

The atlas which Christopher Saxton brought out in 1579 was the first collection of county maps done for England and it was indeed the first to which the idea had been applied.* Christopher Saxton was a topographical artist and a map maker. He was born near Leeds and educated at Cambridge, though at what college is not known. He was flourishing between the years 1570 and 1596, though dates of his birth and death have never been revealed. Saxton undertook on the authority of Queen Elizabeth and at the instigation of Thomas Seckford, Master of Requests and of the Court of Wards, to survey the whole of England and Wales. Seckford obtained for Saxton special facilities from the Privy Council "to be assisted in all places where he shall come for the view of such places to describe certain counties." Travelling in Wales being a matter of difficulty—and not less so because of the language—special instructions were sent to all justices of the peace, mayors, etc., in Wales that Saxton should be "conducted unto any towre, castle, high place or hill to view the countrey and that he may be accompanied with two or three honest men such as do best know the countrey, for the better accomplishment of that service; and at his departure from any towne or place, that he hath taken the view of, the said towne do set forth a horseman that can speke both Welsh and Englishe to safe conduct him to the next market town." Saxton obtained a licence or monopoly to sell his maps for a term of ten years. His atlas, which is now rare, contains thirty-five maps engraved in various years between 1574-78. Separate maps by Saxton are increasingly difficult to obtain and they are far more rarely seen in dealers' lists than are any others. Saxton's atlas was issued with an illuminated and engraved frontispiece, the central figure on which is Queen Elizabeth holding the sceptre and the globe, seated on a throne under an elaborate canopy surmounted by the Royal Arms and two cupids holding laurel crowns. At the right and left there are figures of men with globes and compasses. Most of the maps were engraved by Dutch artists, including Remigius Hogenberg, brother of Francis. Both brothers had come to England about 1560 to do work. In Saxton's maps we see the birth of fine ornament in the borders. On the top of Saxton's map of Somerset, for instance, two cherubs are seen holding up a canopy or drapery and the title is enclosed in an elaborate rectangular cartouche surmounted by the Royal arms and supported by the arms of Scotland and

* Sir G. Fordham.

Ireland. Sailing vessels, whales, etc., are included in Saxton's maps where there is a seaboard county. Owing to the fact that Saxton was a native of Yorkshire he made the map of that county considerably larger than others. Augustine Ryther, a famous map maker, was not only a contemporary of Saxton's but he was a fellow townsman and both hailed from the same neighbourhood. Thoresby said that Saxton's map of Yorkshire was "the best that ever was made of that county." When Ortelius visited England in 1577 and met Camden he persuaded him to write his *Britannia*, and the 1607 edition of Camden's great book contains many of Saxton's and Norden's maps. About 1599 Peter Keir or Kærius issued Saxton's maps in a pocket size.

John Speed who followed Saxton as a map maker of the English counties carried the application of decoration much farther than his predecessor. Speed's maps are attractive and decorative, though he did not add much to our geographical knowledge. He owed much to the Dutch map men and also to Saxton. He shared too with Saxton and Norden the honour of illustrating the 1607 edition of Camden's *Britannia*. Before dealing further with his fine record as a map maker a few biographical facts relating to Speed's career may be included. John Speed was born about 1552 at Farndon in Cheshire. He was brought up to his father's trade of tailoring and he settled in London. Through the generosity of a rich benefactor, Sir Fulke Greville he had a competence. Referring to this assistance Speed proclaims his indebtedness to Greville, "whose merits to me I do acknowledge in setting this hand free from the daily imployment of a manuall trade and giving it full liberty thus to express the inclination of my mind, himself being the procurer of my present estate." There is some reason for believing that Speed first issued his maps separately and that they were collected together in 1611 to form *The Theatre of the Empire of Great Britain*, which was the title of Speed's chief book. A second edition of Speed's *Theatre* appeared in 1614, and a third in 1627 with the title *A Prospect of the most famous parts of the World*. An enlarged edition appeared in 1676, and this is the best one to possess. Between 1605 and 1610 Speed published maps of the English counties, some of which may have been issued before the plates were finished. The cartouches in these are left blank, while in others the engraver's name and date are wanting. The British Museum has a collection of these early impressions. The Dutch influence in Speed is clearly seen and many of his maps are signed Jodocus Hondius and dated 1610.* Others are said to have been engraved by Abraham Goos, another famous Dutch map maker. Speed's maps are rarely found with contemporary colouring. Nearly all Speed maps now sold are coloured skilfully, it is true, but by present day colourists. Each Speed map has many attractive pictorial features, besides showing woods, moors, rivers, bridges, towns, villages and hundreds. Coats-of-arms of prominent local families are included, and the title on each map is in a fine decorative panel. Open compasses are used as a further adornment and the whole map is enclosed in an ornate border. In Speed's maps specially attractive and valuable features are the plans of towns and the portraits. The map of Cambridgeshire has twenty-eight coats-of-arms of the colleges or of the families associated with the county. The Buckinghamshire map has a plan of the Berkshire town of Reading because Speed says he could not find room for it in the map of Berkshire. The Derbyshire map has a plan of the town of Derby with a view of the bathing house at Buxton. Hampshire has a view of Winchester and of Southampton. Speed says of the last named "it is a town populous and rich and beautiful, from whom the whole shire deriveth her name, strongly walled about, having seven gates and twenty-nine Towres for defence, two very stately keys for ships arrivage, and five fair churches for God's divine service." In the edition of *The Theatre of the Empire*, issued in 1676, there are about eleven maps which are of American interest, including the World map on which California is represented as an island, the American continent with ten costume figures, Bermuda with ships and sea monsters, Virginia and Maryland with scroll-work and other adornment, New England and New York with pictures of the bear, the beaver, deer and birds, Jamaica and Barbadoes with ships and sea monsters, and Carolina finished off with numerous ornaments. The 1676 edition of Speed's book contains as well many maps of European countries and of the East.

Richard Blome's maps are very often seen in catalogues. They are the maps which are taken from that compiler's *Britannia*. Blome was originally a ruler of paper and afterwards became an heraldic painter. His maps have many good features, but his whole book *Britannia* is taken from Camden's book of the same name and the maps are largely copied from Speed.

Although England may justly claim to be a pioneer in pro-

* Fordham.

ducing maps of counties, yet France came along soon after, both England and France owing much to Dutch and Flemish assistance. It must be kept in mind that when Ortelius issued his atlas in 1570 entitled *Theatrum Orbis Terrarum,* he included in it a number of maps of the French Provinces. In early editions of Ortelius there were maps of lower Auvergne, the coast of Languedoc, Savoy, part of Burgundy and other districts. But the real starting point in the publication of an atlas of French maps to correspond in any way with Saxton's atlas of the English counties was the publication at Tours in 1594 of Maurice Bouguereau's atlas, *Le Théâtre Français.* Bouguereau was a master printer and publisher of whom very little is known except that he carried on his business at La Petite Fontaine in the old town of Tours. Bouguereau followed much the same plan as most of the early map makers had done, for he made free use of maps already existing and the maps of Ortelius and others were borrowed from, but Bouguereau employed a good engraver, one Gabriel Tavernier, for executing many of the maps in his atlas. His work *Le Théâtre Français* is now one of the rarest of all the early atlases and very few copies can be traced, though three at least of the existing copies are in England.* As early as April, 1591 (the atlas was not issued complete until 1594), Bouguereau is found presenting an illuminated and decorated copy of his map of Touraine to the municipality of Tours and he was assisted in his work from the municipal chest. Ornamental borders, heraldic coats-of-arms, compasses and other instruments decorate the maps in this first atlas of the provinces of France.*

Of those who followed Bouguereau the next is Le Clerc, who made use of Bouguereau's plates but added others of his own. The Le Clercs, father and son, produced atlases of France in 1620 with thirty-nine maps, in 1621 with forty-five maps, in 1626 with forty-nine maps, and in 1632 with fifty-five maps.*

Melchior Tavernier followed, publishing in 1634 *Le Théâtre Géographique du Royaume de France,* the maps in which book are many of them taken from Jodocus and Henricus Hondius, Jansson and Blaeu, as well as a number from Le Clerc. A good description of Tavernier's atlas is given in Phillips, IV., p. 462. After Tavernier there came the most famous of the French topographical map makers. This was Nicholas Sanson, who was born at Abbeville in 1600 and died in Paris in 1667. Sanson published more than three hundred maps and many of the earliest

* Fordham.

of these are in the British Museum. Sanson's maps deal with many parts of the world, several being of America. The French atlases of Hubert Alexis Jaillot and Nicholas Sanson are important productions and stand well amid many rivals. A list of those which deal with the French provinces is given in Fordham's *Cartography of the French Provinces,* p. 161 (See also Phillips, i., 234-5 and iv. 127). Finally, the great atlas issued as late as 1757 by Vaugondy in Paris and called *Atlas Universel* closes the series of French provincial atlases. The elder Sanson, who died in 1667, left about four hundred plates to his sons, who kept up the name. Subsequently their stock came into the hands of Robert Vaugondy. Vaugondy's maps have ornamental panels or cartouches and the titles of the maps are done with that delicacy of ornamentation which characterised French art at this period. Surveying the maps produced in delineation of the French provinces, Sir George Fordham singles out the map of Picardy of 1592 engraved by Gabriel Tavernier, which, although it may not be French in its origin yet in its art may be considered as typical of the progress of cartography in the latter part of the sixteenth century. Sanson's map of the South East of England and of Picardy (1654) are good specimens of his work and of the Abbeville engravers he employed. A detailed description of Sanson's atlas may be found in Phillips, iii., p. 228. It was through the fine work executed by him that French eminence in cartographic art was attained, and the reputation of the family of Sanson as map makers was kept up by Nicholas Sanson's sons Nicholas, Adrien and Guillaume, all of whom worked with Hubert Jaillot (1681-1717), Pierre Duval (1619-1683), and J. B. Nolin (1692) at the French book of charts, *Le Neptune François* (1693).

A list of the royal geographers of France will often serve in fixing the dates of the many undated maps of this period. Such a list is given from 1560 in the *Bulletin de la Société Geographique d'Anvers,* i., 477, and includes :—

Nicholas Sanson, in office, 1647-1667.
P. Duval, 1664-1667.
Adrien Sanson, first son of Nicholas, 1667.
Guillaume Sanson, second son of Nicholas, 1667.
Jean B. d'Anville (b. 1697 ; d. 1782), 1718.
Guillaume Delisle (b. 1675 ; d. 1726), 1718.
Jean de Beaurain (b. 1696 ; d. 1771), 1721.
Le Rouge, 1722.

Philip Buache, d. 1773.
Roussel, 1730.
Hubert Jaillot, 1736.
Bernard Jaillot, 1736.
Robert de Vaugondy (b. 1688; d. 1766), 1760.

I must now return to Holland and Flanders. I have pointed out the height to which map making rose in Europe under Blaeu's great influence, ability and enterprise. All who acquire even a slight acquaintance with the maps issued by Blaeu will see how excellent in technique and in methods of production they are, and time seems to have had but little effect in dimming their brilliance of colour and quality. A history of the families and firms engaged on Dutch map engraving and publishing is one well worth putting together. We have seen how Jodocus Hondius succeeded to the business of his brother-in-law, R. Mercator, and how Henricus Hondius, the son of Jodocus was followed by his brother-in-law, Jansson. There were many other connections besides these in the map producing fraternity. We know, for instance, that F. de Wit purchased the plates which escaped the great fire at the Blaeus. De Wit then started as an engraver of maps, his firm lasting until 1712. The Hogenberg family was another which had come in at the start of atlas making when Abraham Hogenberg assisted in engraving the plates for the first atlas of Ortelius, *Theatrum Orbis Terrarum*. The Hogenberg family were early Flemish engravers going back to Henry Hogenberg the elder, who was born at Mechlin about 1500. Of the Hoefnagle family I have already said a good deal. Yet another family of Flemings were the de Jodes, a numerous family almost wholly employed in engraving. Gerard de Jode published about 1578 an Atlas called *Speculum Orbis Terrarum* which contained early maps of the French Provinces. The Tavernier family, too, from Antwerp established themselves in Paris as engravers and publishers of maps. Augustine Ryther, whose name appears on many maps as engraver, although his name has so foreign a sound, was an Englishman, a print dealer and engraver who had his shop "a little way from Leadenhall, near the sign of the Tower." He did good work in engraving plates of the Spanish Fleet at the time of the Armada and, as I have already said, he assisted his friend and fellow Yorkshireman in executing maps of the English counties. One of the oldest and largest of map producing families in Amsterdam were the Visschers. In the middle of the sixteenth century Jan C.

Visscher carried on a print selling business in Amsterdam. Some of the maps in the earlier of the Blaeu atlases bear the name of Nicholas Joannis Visscher. N. J. Visscher was succeeded by his son Nicholas who produced many atlases. (For notes on the Visscher family see Phillips, iii., 164). The elder Visscher flourished between 1621 and 1670 and the younger died in 1709.

With the close of the seventeenth century the influence of the Dutch school ended. Nicholas Visscher's plates eventually became the property of Peter Schenck. To write of the decline of any of the arts is not a cheerful part of one's work, but yet it has to be done. As surely as map making became a lucrative business not only did its scientific value decrease but its artistic touches gradually disappeared, and in the hands of the later Visschers, of F. de Wit and his son, and of Peter Schenck, there was a definite decline in beauty. The atlases by Visscher are numerous and they were, like most seventeenth century atlases, made up of collections of maps. In almost any of Visscher's atlases we find maps by Ortelius, Sanson, Blaeu and Jansson. Their American interest is not slight, and most of Visscher's atlases have a dozen or more maps of North and South America. Lists of the maps in Visscher's chief Atlases are given in Phillips, vol. iii., pp. 164, 223.

When Peter Schenck took over much of Visscher's plant he added to them and changed the character of the atlases. Peter Schenck (1645-1715) was an engraver and a publisher but his atlases contain more than mere maps. They are picture books. It was part of Schenck's business to publish views of cities. His energies as a publisher were great and covered a wide field of work. His *Hecatomopolis* contains many fine views of European towns. Several of his volumes contain battle scenes. (For a description of his 1705 atlas see Phillips, iii., 247). Another family of map producers in Amsterdam were the De Wits, father, son and uncle, and between them they issued three hundred and eighty maps and thirty sea-charts. The De Wits, unlike most Amsterdam houses, had a London imprint as well as their own. "Sold by Christopher Browne at ye Globe at the westend of St. Paulls church" appears on some of De Wit's maps. Christopher Browne was well known in connection with the publication of important English maps including those by Sir Jonas Moore. But little original work marks the many other map publishers of the later period. De Lisle, Ottens, Homann, stand out possibly above many others, but all these were engaged in collecting maps together from every source they could and issuing them in the form of atlases. De Lisle's Atlas of 1730 (see Phillips, iii., 325) contains an important map of Paris and about a dozen maps of American interest. The atlases by Ottens were produced by a firm in Amsterdam (R. & J. Ottens, 1703-1756) and contain maps by Jaillot, Sanson and Visscher. Johann Baptist Homann (1664-1724) is among the later map publishers and he produced in Nuremberg some finely engraved maps with colouring and ornamentation. These obtained a wide sale in the eighteenth century and are often found in English libraries.

In 1680-82 an English rival appeared on the scene in Moses Pitt. The son of a Cornish yeoman of St. Teath, he came to London about 1654 and served as an apprentice in a city business. In 1668 he began to publish books and in 1680 there appeared the one publication by which Pitt will be remembered—*The English Atlas,* a work of great splendour with maps upon which neither gold nor colour had been spared. The influence of the Dutch is clearly seen. Many of Pitt's maps were based upon Jansson's Atlas. *The English Atlas* was to have extended to eleven volumes but only four appeared. It was a commercial failure and Pitt got imprisoned for debt over the publisher's costs. Fine copies occasionally turn up, but rarely all four volumes together. If in good condition they should always be purchased.

Certain Dutch map men, finding perhaps the market in Amsterdam for maps overdone, came over to London to try their fortunes. Among these were Hermann Moll and one of the Mortier family. Moll came over to London about 1698 and set up "over against Devereux Court between Temple Bar and St. Clements Church in the Strand." Although Moll belongs to the period of decline his maps contain many fine emblematic designs with pictures of richly dressed figures of natives or scenes in which sport predominates. Moll had no doubt earlier in life in Amsterdam seen and known much of the methods of borrowing maps one from another, so when he was established in London he was disposed to make use of this knowledge to enlarge the beam in his brother cartographer's eye. "The world," said he, "is nothing more scandalously imposed upon than by maps put out by ignorant pretenders nor are we cheated only by these pretenders at home but by others from abroad who are encouraged to publish every wretched coppy that falls into their hands." On Moll's South Sea Company map of 1715 we find the following printed: "There is lately published a two sheet map of South

America coppied after a very erroneous French map done in Paris in 1703 and to deceive the world dedicated to Dr. Halley and pretended in ye dedication to be corrected by his own discoveries." Moll utters a warning against Sanson's maps. He says that the French cartographer is "notoriously false" and he adds "as for ye Dutch maps all of 'em yet extant are much alike and far enough from correctness. Now it being a great hazard we run in undertakings of this nature and are labouring under ye frequent hardships of having our maps copy[d] upon us in Holland ....brought over better, publickly advertised and sold under other names to their profit and to ye manifest defrauding of us as well in point of reputation or otherwise."*

John Senex, who died in 1740, had a map seller's establishment at the Globe in Salisbury Court, Fleet Street. He printed in conjunction with C. Price, *Proposals for a new sett of correct mapps*. In 1714 appeared his *English Atlas*. On one of his maps at this date (1714) he says that all maps printed for H. Jaillot and P. Mortier and brought to England for correct maps are only copies from Sanson with all his errors and several of them added not to be found in Sanson.

I have up to now omitted to say anything about the numerous sea-atlases which were a great feature in map production at the close of the sixteenth century and onwards. In the year 1584 and only a few years after the first great land atlas had been issued by Ortelius it occurred to a remarkable navigator named Lucas Janszoon Wagenar to publish an atlas of sea-charts. It was published through the great firm of Plantin at their Leyden house with twenty-three maps engraved on copper. The text was in Dutch. Later editions were issued containing forty-four sea maps and charts. Wagenar was a native of Enchuysen (Enkhuizen) in Holland, and was born there about 1550. He served in the Dutch merchant service in his boyhood and he became one of the most famous and most skilful pilots of his time. Wagenar's work soon obtained a great reputation among seafaring men. The author did not set out to publish a beautiful or artistic book. His object was to bring out a practical atlas for travellers and navigators. His book called *The Mariner's Mirror,* now very rare, is brimming over with knowledge of navigation and may still be used to some purpose by yachtsmen and sailors. Soon after the publication at Leyden of this notable sea atlas, the Armada came, and Lord Effingham having already

* Holman, *Old Maps*, Boston, 1925.

drawn the attention of the Privy Council to the great value of Wagenar's work, the book was at once "esteemed by the chief personages of the grave counsell worthy to be translated and printed into a language familiar to all nations." The task of translating it into English from the Dutch was given to Anthony Ashley, a member of the ancient family which has been settled in Dorset since the days of Henry VI. The title-page of the English edition is reproduced among our illustrations.

The maps in Wagenar are of special interest, being classed among the earliest specimens of copper-plate engraving in England. Such rare books as Linschoten's *Itinerary,* 1599, and the books of De Bry contain similarly engraved plates belonging to the Wagenar period. Wagenar is sometimes found coloured. All the maps and charts are elaborately designed with ornamental cartouches, ships, fish and fishing boats. The engravers of the maps were, among others, Jodocus Hondius, Johannes Rutlinger and Augustine Ryther, who was busily engaged about this time in engraving designs illustrating the Spanish fleet. The English edition is in black letter small folio size. It is not altogether surprising that the name of the author became corrupted into "Waggoner," and after the Armada and throughout the seventeenth century the book was always referred to as a "Waggoner." Thus Pepys under date July 22, 1663, writes "Thence to my booksellers and found my Waggoners done. The very binding cost me 14/- but they are well done and so with a porter home with them." Again, on September 19th, 1666, he writes: "mightily troubled even in my sleep at my missing four or five of my biggest books, Speeds chronicle and maps and the two parts of Waggoner which I suppose I have put up with too much care that I have forgot where they are for sure they are not stole." Nordenskiöld in his *Facsimile Atlas* states that he considers a new period in the history of sailing directions as well as in that of charts begins with Lucas Janszoon Wagenar and he adds: "this work is the finest collection of sea charts published in print." It was much appreciated among the seafaring nations of Europe and published in a number of editions in various languages. Nordenskiöld points out what is no doubt perfectly correct that Wagenar's book was based on Italian or Catalan portolans and on ancient sailing directions for the Baltic. A full list of the charts in Wagenar is given in Phillips, iii., pp. 611-614.

One of the earliest and rarest of marine atlases is Sir Robert Dudley's *Dell' Arcano del Mare, 1646-7.* This is the first sea atlas in which the maps were drawn on the Mercator projection. The author, Sir Robert Dudley, son of the Earl of Leicester, was well qualified by travel and the possession of new material to produce a work of lasting value. His knowledge gained through his experience as a seaman, together with that of his brother-in-law, Henry Cavendish, the navigator, is fully set forth and accompanied by additional information supplied by Absalom Kendal and Colin Davis. The manuscript of the original work is in the Royal Library at Munich. The engraver, Antonio Francesco Lucini, states in the dedicatory epistle to the second edition, 1661, that he worked on the plates in seclusion for twelve years in an obscure Tuscan village, using no less than 5,000 pounds of copper in the making. The lettering used on the maps is in a particularly beautiful and unique hand, highly decorative and ornamental.

As far as beauty and decorative value go in sea atlases the maps issued by Peter Goos are superior to others. Peter Goos was one of the best of the Amsterdam school and he had learned much from Blaeu. His maps are brilliant in colouring and are adorned with figures of Venus, Bacchus, cupids and symbols of plenty as well as many heraldic shields. The Goos family were at the height of their skill between 1656-1692. A rival to Goos in the issuing of sea maps was Hendrick Doncker. The first edition of Hendrick Doncker's *Zee-Atlas* appeared at Amsterdam in 1659 and is particularly useful for the American coasts. New maps were added to it in the edition of 1666; but the *Nieuwe Groote vermeerderde Zee Atlas* of 1676, though still called Doncker's, is based on Colom, and has Colom's six American charts. Additional American and other charts were added to the 1697 edition; while a set of still larger charts constitutes *Doncker's Nieuw Groot Zeekaertboek* of 1712.

The Van Keulen firm were in full swing as a great nautical firm a few years later and they issued two or more big sea atlases, the one of 1696 having eleven maps bearing on America. The remaining sea atlases are those of Van Loon, Seller, Greenvile Collins and Thornton.

The *Zee-Atlas* of Van Loon, with its forty-five double charts, appeared in 1661. It is in part reproduced from Blaeu, De Laet and Jansson. P. Goos, in his *Lichtende Colomne,* Amsterdam, 1657, had touched the Arctic coasts of America, but in his *Zee-Atlas* of 1666 he gave in excellent manner eleven charts of the coasts of both Americas, out of the forty-one charts in all. These were all repeated in the edition of 1668-1669, and in the French edition, *Atlas de la Mer,* 1673. Other Dutch editions with some changes followed in 1675 and 1676. It was issued with an English text at Amsterdam in 1670.

Seller was publisher of maps, charts and geographical books in which he seems to have tried to make a corner. He flourished round and about 1700 and was for some years in business at The Hermitage in Wapping, where no doubt he did direct business with the mariners. John Seller, junior, had a shop at The Sign of The Star near Mercer's Chapel in Cheapside, where the elder Seller's publications could be bought. Greenvile Collins (flourished 1679-1693) was a captain in the Navy. In 1681 he was ordered to survey and chart the coasts of the Kingdom and in 1693 the full results were issued in *Great Britain's Coasting Pilot*. Of Thornton less is known. He issued in 1716 *the English Pilot* and earlier he had published his *Atlas Maritimus* in which there are several maps of American interest. All these English sea atlases belong to the period when decoration in maps had greatly declined, and although the maps are of interest and value they are for the most part coarsely and heavily drawn and they lack charm.

No work on decorative maps could omit to notice the magnificent tapestry maps which now hang in the Victoria and Albert Museum at South Kensington. These fine maps represent the best work put forth by the hand looms set up by William Sheldon at Weston and Barchester in Warwickshire. The Sheldon family for several generations were magnificent patrons of learning. These tapestry maps, which everyone should see, were woven in the later years of the sixteenth century and the earlier years of the seventeenth. Horace Walpole bought four of the great Sheldon maps and gave three of them to Lady Harcourt, who had a special room built for them at Nuneham. Their full story is told in a scholarly and lucid way and accompanied by many facsimiles in a pamphlet handbook issued and sold at the Victoria and Albert Museum. The maps themselves are presumably on loan and are now hung on the walls at South Kensington. They include Worcestershire, Oxfordshire, Berkshire, Gloucestershire, Warwickshire and London and the district around.

It is not surprising that we find numerous references to maps in English literature dating from the days of Ortelius and

Mercator and onwards shewing the importance which was attached to a knowledge of maps. A map to an Elizabethan was a thing that stirred his imagination. Thomas Blundeville, a Norfolk squire, for instance, a man devoted chiefly to horses and to sport, found time and inclination to write and to publish in 1589 a small dumpy black letter volume called *A Brief description of Universal mappes and cardes and of their use and also the use of Phtolemey his tables*. The first use of the word " carde " in the sense of a map or plan was in 1527. It occurs in Hakluyt's *Divers Voyages*, 1582, in the sentence "a little map or carde of the world."

Henry Bynneman, a London publisher and famous printer of Elizabethan days, was making a bid to secure the growing map business in his day when he printed in 1573 *Certaine briefe rules of geographie serving for the understanding of maps and charts.* When that fantastic person, Robert Burton, published in 1621 his *Anatomy of Melancholy* he suggests as an antidote to depression the study of maps. " What greater pleasure," says Burton, " can there now be than to view those elaborate maps of Ortelius and Mercator and to peruse those books of cities put out by Braunus and Hogenbergius." As early as 1559 Dr. William Cunningham, a doctor of Norwich, published *The Cosmographical Glasse, conteinyng the pleasant principles of cosmographie, geographie, hydrographie or navigation.* This book contains a plan of Norwich as it was in 1558. Cunningham says that he was " the first that ever in one tongue hath written of this argument."

Speed's maps were favourites with Pepys. Under date September 26, 1660, he enters in his Diary : " In the evening to the office where I fell a reading of Speed's Geography for awhile." Two years later he takes up Speed again to find out all he could about the Forest of Dean and Speed did not fail to tell him what he sought. John Evelyn was for introducing improved methods in maps and he read a paper before the Royal Society, "Of a method of making more lively representations of nature in wax than are extant in painting, and of a new kind of maps in bas relief; both practised in France."

Swift saw some fun to be made of the ornament used in seventeenth century maps and wrote :—

> " So geographers in Afric's maps
> With savage pictures fill their gaps
> And o'er unhabitable downs
> Place elephants for want of towns."

About the year of the Restoration a small folio volume was issued which clearly reveals the interest taken in maps and in the colouring of them. This book was called *Albert Durer revived; or a book of drawing, limning, washing or colouring of maps and prints and the art of Painting.* It contains a mass of recipes, many of which are no doubt of practical value. It was, however, left to John Smith, clockmaker, to issue *The Art of Painting in oyl to which is added the whole art and mystery of colouring maps.* Various editions exist all dated about 1700. John Smith is believed originally to have been a blacksmith and tool maker. He was a Unitarian also, which led him to plunge into theological discussions when his antagonist advised him to return to the noise of his hammer and the use of his pincers. He died before 1730, at which date it was advertised that his books could be obtained of "Mary Smith at the Fan and Flower de Luce over against Somerset House in the Strand and nowhere else." The little volume on the colouring of maps is, as far as I am aware, the only treatise in which there is "a special chapter on map colouring." I shall therefore reprint it here.

"The colours being prepared you may proceed to colour a map in this manner; first take notice of the several divisions in a map which distinguish one kingdom from another, or one county from another, which are known by certain lines or rows of pricks, or points of several sizes and shapes, agreeable to the divisions they are to denote. As for instance, Portugal is distinguished from Spain by a row of large points, or pricks, and the provinces of that kingdom, or shires, as we call them in England, are distinguished one from another by lines of lesser points or pricks. Now if you were to colour the kingdom of Portugal, do thus: first with a small camel-hair pencil in a duck's quill, colour over all the hills within the large pricked line that divides it from Spain, with the tincture of myrrh, very thin; then, if there be any woods, dab every tree with the point of a very fine pencil dipped in grass-green, made of copper-green, tempered up with gumboge; but in dipping your pencil into any colour, stroke it against the sides of the pot or glass in which you put it, that the colour may not drop from it and spoil your work; then, with another pencil dipped in red lead, tempered thinly with gum-water, let the principal cities and towns be done over, that the eye may more readily perceive them. Lastly, with a duck's quill pencil dipped in copper-green, trace out the bounds of one of the provinces, keeping the outmost edge of the pencil close to the pricks; and be careful to lay your colours all alike, and not thick in one place and thin in another, or too deep in some places and too light in others; and when it is almost dry, take another clean pencil of the same size, and dip it in water, stroking the water out well, and therewith rub upon the inside of the coloured line, till it take away most of the colour on the edge, and make it grow faint and lose itself by degrees, and continue so to do till you have gone quite round; then take yellow made of gumboge, and go round the inside of the pricks that divide the next province, sweetening over the innermost side of it. When almost dry, with a pencil dipped in water, as you did before, do over the next to that with the crimson tincture made with cochineal and the next do round with red-lead, and the next to that with grass-green, and the next to that with any of the former colours that will so agree with the work, that two adjoining provinces may not be coloured with the same colour, for then you could not distinguish them. And in this work of dividing observe, that when your boundary lines pass through woods already coloured, or hills; observe then, I say, to miss those woods and hills in your drawing a colour round the province; and be careful also not to draw any colour over the cities or towns that are painted red, for that spoils the beauty.

"And when you have coloured over or divided all the counties, then colour the sea-shore, and all lakes of water, if there be any, with thin indigo, working on that side of the colour, which is from the land, faint, with a wet pencil as before taught; and, if there be any ships, colour the water shaded at the bottom with the same indigo, painting the hull of the ship with umber, the sails with tincture of myrrh, and the flags with vermilion or blue-bice; and, if they are represented as firing their guns, let all the smoke be done with very thin bice; and as for the margent, or square stick of degrees, as the gravers term it, which goes round the map, let that be coloured either with yellow or red-lead, or crimson; none but those three colours serving well for this purpose.

"As for the compartment or title, which consists generally of some neat device to set the map off, and make it appear more beautiful, it may be coloured according to the nature of it. As for instance; crowns, or anything representing gold, with yellow, shadowed in the darkest parts of the graving with orpiment; the hair of men or women with tincture of myrrh, or if black, with half water half common ink or with burned umber; the flesh of women or boys, with a very little of the tincture of cochineal, in a large quantity of water; and garments either with thin green, shadowed with thicker, and with the tincture of cochineal made thin with water, and shaded with the same colour thicker, and thin bice, and shadowed with a thicker mixture of the same, or with vermilion shaded with carmine. In general observe, that the thinner the colour is laid in the lightest part of all garments, and the deeper in the shades, the more beautiful it appears; for the thick of the same colour is the most natural shade for most colours, except yellow and blue; for blue sometimes requires to be shaded in the darkest places with a black, or at least with thick indigo; and yellow requires red lead or crimson.

"If you are to paint clouds, do them sometimes with tincture of myrrh; and in some cases with a very thin crimson; and, for variety, you may do some with thin ivory-black, ground very fine, and tempered up with much gum-water. Smoke is best represented with very thin blue-bice, and if you are to colour any representation of sea-waves, do it with indigo.

"If you are to colour any representations of land, do the lightest parts over with very thin yellow, that represents a straw colour, shading it with orpiment; and in other parts, do it with light green and shade it with a deeper green.

"Rocks must be done with tincture of myrrh, and the trees, some with copper-green, some with dark grass-green, and some with thin umber. Houses may be done with red-lead, and the tiles with vermilion or with bice, to represent blue slate; castles may be done with tincture of myrrh in some parts, in others, with thin red-lead; and the spires and pinnacles with blue.

"But when all is said that can be said, the only way to colour maps well, is by a patern done by some good workman, of which the Dutch are esteemed the best. Three of four such maps, coloured by a good artist, are sufficient to guide a man in the right doing of his work; but, if he cannot obtain this, he may, by a few trials, grow a good artist in a short time; and if a man does spoil half a score maps, in order to get the knack of colouring a map well at last, there is no man that is ingenious will grumble at it.

"The art of colouring well may be attained to by practice, as was said; but the hardest thing is to know rightly how to make and prepare the colours, which is here taught faithfully; and if your paper be good, and bear the colours well, without suffering them to sink into it, all that are here mentioned will lie fair and pleasant to the eye; and it is the fairness of the colours that is most esteemed in this art of map-painting; but if the paper be not good and strong, no art can make the colours lie well; therefore in buying maps, chuse those that are printed on the strongest or thickest paper."

The Art of Painting in Oil. By John Smith. 9th. edn. London 1788. pp. 106-112. Of the practice of Colouring Maps.

With the publication of Cary's maps our story must end, because maps were no longer decorated to any extent. The family of Cary established themselves in the Strand at the corner of Arundel Street about the year 1785, and produced a large number of important maps (See Fordham's monograph on Cary). A name equally or perhaps better known in modern map making is that of Arrowsmith. Aaron Arrowsmith (1750-1823) found employment first with Cary and then blossomed out for himself. With the introducing of more precise and scientific methods of surveying there was certainly a loss of beauty. To-day there is room for maps which combine accuracy, symbolism and colour in a way hardly dreamed of even by the great Dutch Cartographers.

Values of old maps and atlases have risen rapidly during the past ten years and specially have they advanced during the last three years. In the sale of Lord Amherst of Hackney's library in 1909 a collection of Ptolemy's were sold and realised from

£6. 15. 0 to £55 each, according to date. Lord Amherst was a connoisseur and many of these were collectors' copies; the prices therefore were high for the date (1909) when they were sold. In other sales the 1475 edition of Ptolemy (*Cosmographia*) realised £14. 15. 0 in 1896, and in 1909, £24. 0. 0., and in 1922, £65.

Wagenar's *Mariner's Mirror,* the earliest book to mention the Spanish Armada, and published in the year 1588, has varied in value chiefly because of the varying condition or completeness of the few copies sold. The book is not often found complete. In 1905 a fine copy bound by Riviere realised £25. 10. 0, an imperfect copy fetched £7. 5. 0 in 1909, and in 1922 another copy realised £11. A perfect copy if sold to-day would realise from £80 to £100 at least, and more if coloured. An Ortelius of 1570 was sold in 1901 for £14 and a copy of the 1595 edition with a few added maps was sold this year (1926) for £320. Mercator's Atlas of 1595 fetched £1. 15. 0 in 1899, and the 1633 edition £16. 10. 0 in 1923.

Braun and Hogenberg's *Civitates Orbis Terrarum* (1572-1618) has varied much in value, chiefly because the book is so seldom found with all the plans. In 1899 a copy realised £3. 7. 6 and in 1901 another copy was sold for £9. 0. 0.; in 1913 a copy fetched £15. 0. 0. A fine coloured and complete copy would be worth at least £75. In 1881 the Comerford copy realised £13. 13. 0.

Blaeu's *Atlas Major* has risen more rapidly than almost any other atlas. In 1911 a coloured copy was sold for £1. 12. 0. In 1922 a copy realised £67, and in 1923 another copy, large paper, realised also £67. A finely bound Blaeu Atlas dated 1648-65 was sold this year (1926) for £320. The famous Dutch Sea Atlas by Goos dated 1668, was sold in 1899 for £3. 6. 0. A copy coloured would to-day realise £70.

Saxton's English County Atlas is one of those which have for many years realised a high price. The fact that Saxton's maps are among the earliest decorative maps and that his book is the first collection of maps of counties, has made it a rare book. Even at the Nassau sale as far back as 1814 a copy realised £8. 5. 0. Then after a long interval a copy was sold in 1895 for £51. Again in 1908 a copy was sold for the same sum. Prices since then have varied much, of course depending on condition, state of colouring and completeness. The portrait of Queen Elizabeth is often missing. A copy without the portrait realised £188 this year (1926).

Speed's Atlas, *The Theatre of the Empire,* dated 1676, which is the best edition with American maps, was thought of little account in 1829, for in the Hibbert Sale which took place in that year a copy fetched 18/- only. From 1898 to 1923 copies varied in value, realising from £3 to £5 each. In 1923 a copy belonging to William Hewer, the friend of Pepys, with his book-plate, fetched only £5. 10. 0. It is in the last three years that Speed has risen by leaps and bounds. A plain copy would now realise £50 and a contemporary coloured copy would cost at least £150.

The change in value of single maps is remarkable. In the days of John Russell Smith, a great and honest dealer in topography, Saxton's maps were priced by him at 1/6 and Speed's at the same price. About the same time another dealer, not quite so satisfactory in his prices, asked 4/6 for Saxton's maps and 3/- for Blaeu's coloured. As late as 1909 nearly all London dealers were selling Blaeu's, Speed's and Saxton's maps of the counties at 3/6 each, and Blome's were going at 2/6.

THE PLATES

The Ptolemaic World, 1482

From the first edition of Claudius Ptolemy's 'Geographia' to be published north of the alps, at Ulm. This is also the first series to be cut on woodlock as opposed to copperplate and the first likely to be found in contemporary colour. Additionally, this is the first printed map to have the artist's signature – Johannes of Arnsheim – cut in the top border.

The map shows the typical Ptolemaic concept of ancient world geography – a landlocked Indian Ocean, detail fading away from Europe; but this is the first world map to incorporate new information regarding northern European regions.

The New World, 1570

Ortelius' map of North and South America is one of the most famous of all cartographic images. In 1587 Ortelius revised the map and removed South America's prominent 'bulge'.

Scandinavia and the North Atlantic, 1570

Ortelius' map of this region is a delicately designed piece incorporating a musical sea monster, ships, a whale and other beasts. The 'unknown' nature of the area is further reflected by the various 'mythical' islands – Frisland being the largest – and such legends as 'Pigmei hic habitant' on the Arctic landmap 'Pygmies live here'.

South East Asia, 1570

Ortelius' map of this area is one of the most interesting in his atlas. Although the general outlines and locations are good for the period, Japan is shown in one of its most curious forms. The unknown coastlines of Java and New Guinea extend southwards and the name 'Beach' at the bottom of the map is taken from Marco Polo's reports of a great southern continent of that name.

Lᴏɴᴅᴏɴ, 1572

Georg Braun and Frans Hogenberg produced together the 'Ciritates Orbis Terrarum'. A magnificent six volume publication of 548 maps, plans and oblique 'birds-eye views' showing the major cities of all parts of the world. The six volumes appeared between 1572 and 1617. This map, like many others in the publication, is the first printed representation of the city.

ENGLAND AND WALES, 1573

Ortelius used this map by the Welshman Humphrey Lloyd in the *Theatrum*. . . throughout all subsequent editions.

HAMPSHIRE, 1579

Christopher Saxton's atlas of England and Wales, based on maps produced during the preceding several years, was the first national atlas ever published. Saxton employed several engravers to produce his maps including, in this instance, Leonard Terwoort.

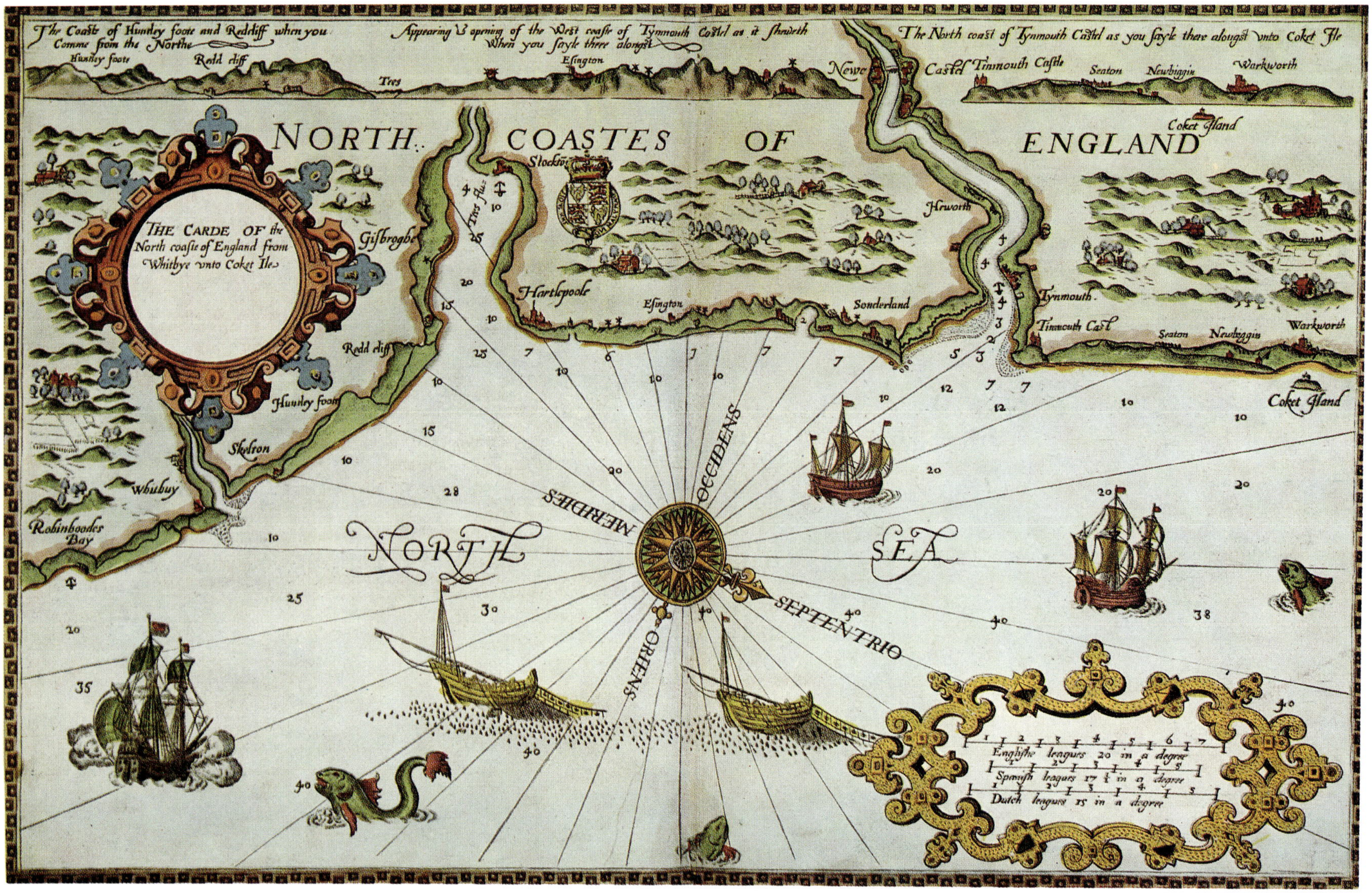

ENGLAND'S NORTH EAST COAST, 1588

This and the subsequent charts are from Waghenaer's great sea chart book (see previous description). Covering the coasts from Robin Hood's Bay at Whitby, Yorkshire to Cocket Island, Northumberland, the chart is decorated amply within the sea areas while coastal profiles and inland features that are visible from sea are identified.

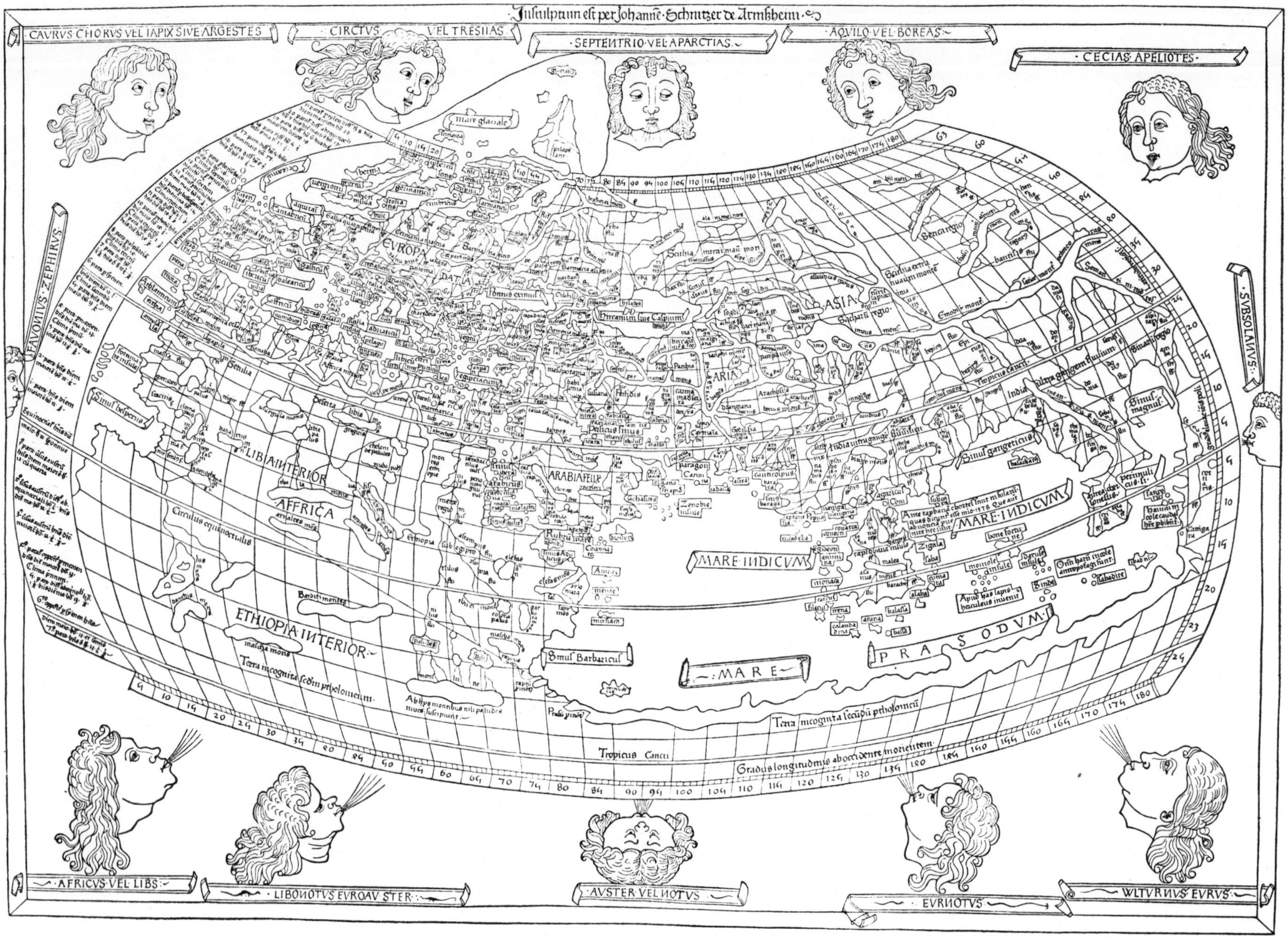

THE WORLD. ENGRAVED BY JOHANNES SCHNITZER DE ARMSSHEIM.
(Ptolemy, Cosmographia, *Ulm*, 1482.)

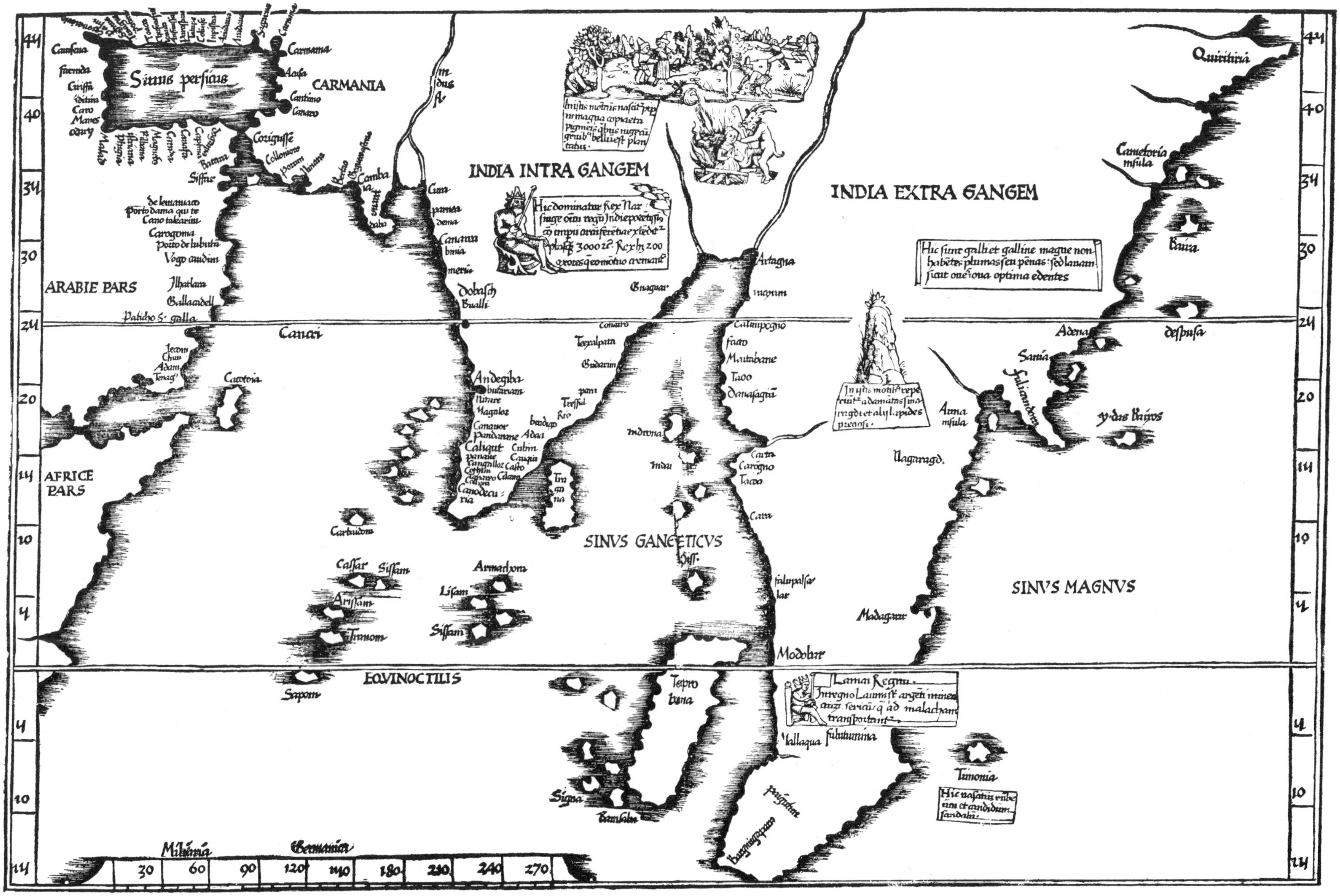

INDIA.

(Ptolemy, "Geographicæ Enarrationis, Etc." 1535.)

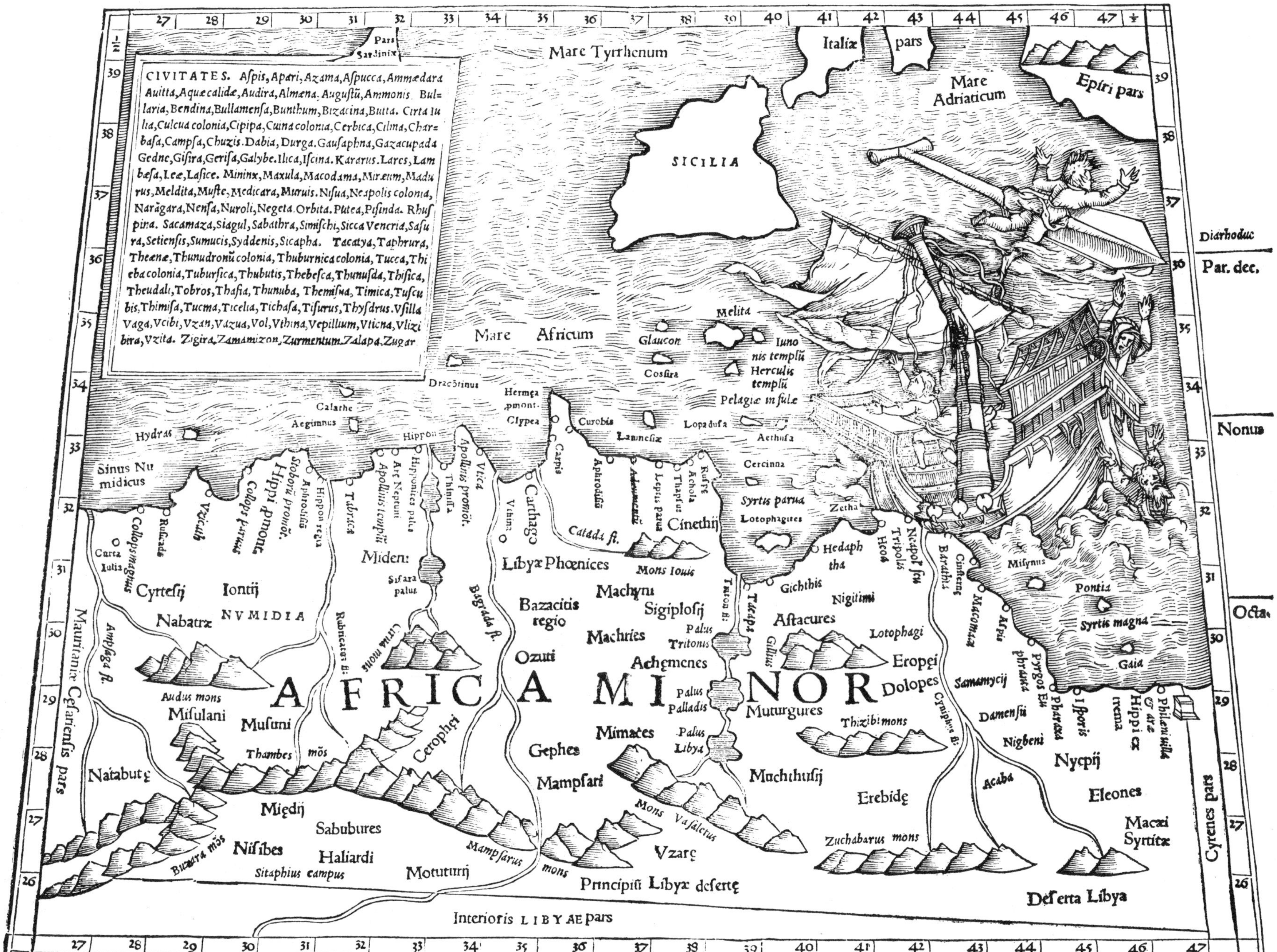

AFRICA MINOR.
(PTOLEMY, "GEOGRAPHIA UNIVERSALIS," 1540.)

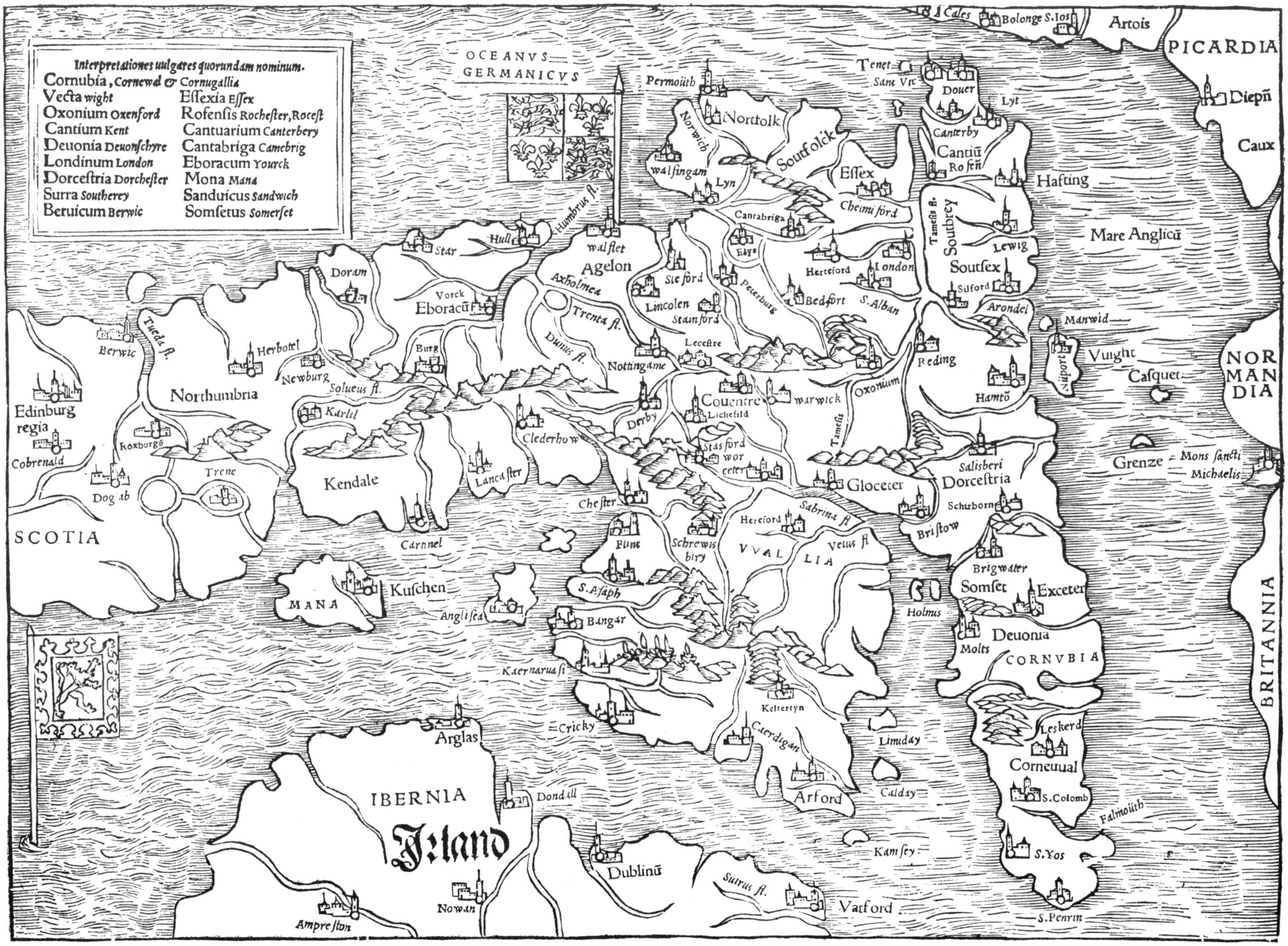

ENGLAND.
(Ptolemy, "Geographia Universalis," 1540.)

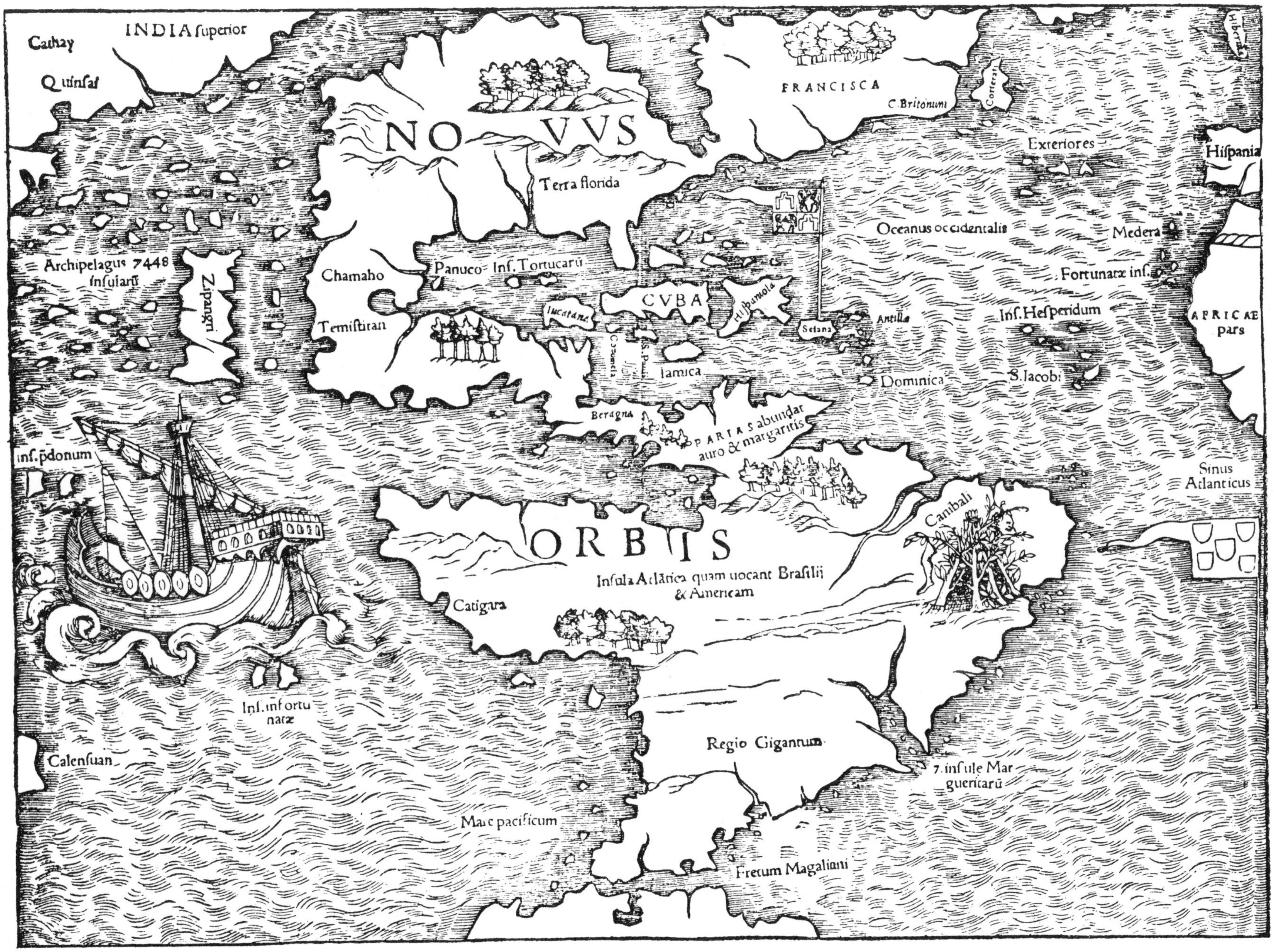

THE NEW WORLD.
(PTOLEMY, "GEOGRAPHIA UNIVERSALIS," 1540.)

CHARTA COSMOGRAPHICA, CUM VENTORUM, ETC.
(PETER APIANUS, "COSMOGRAPHIA," 1545.)

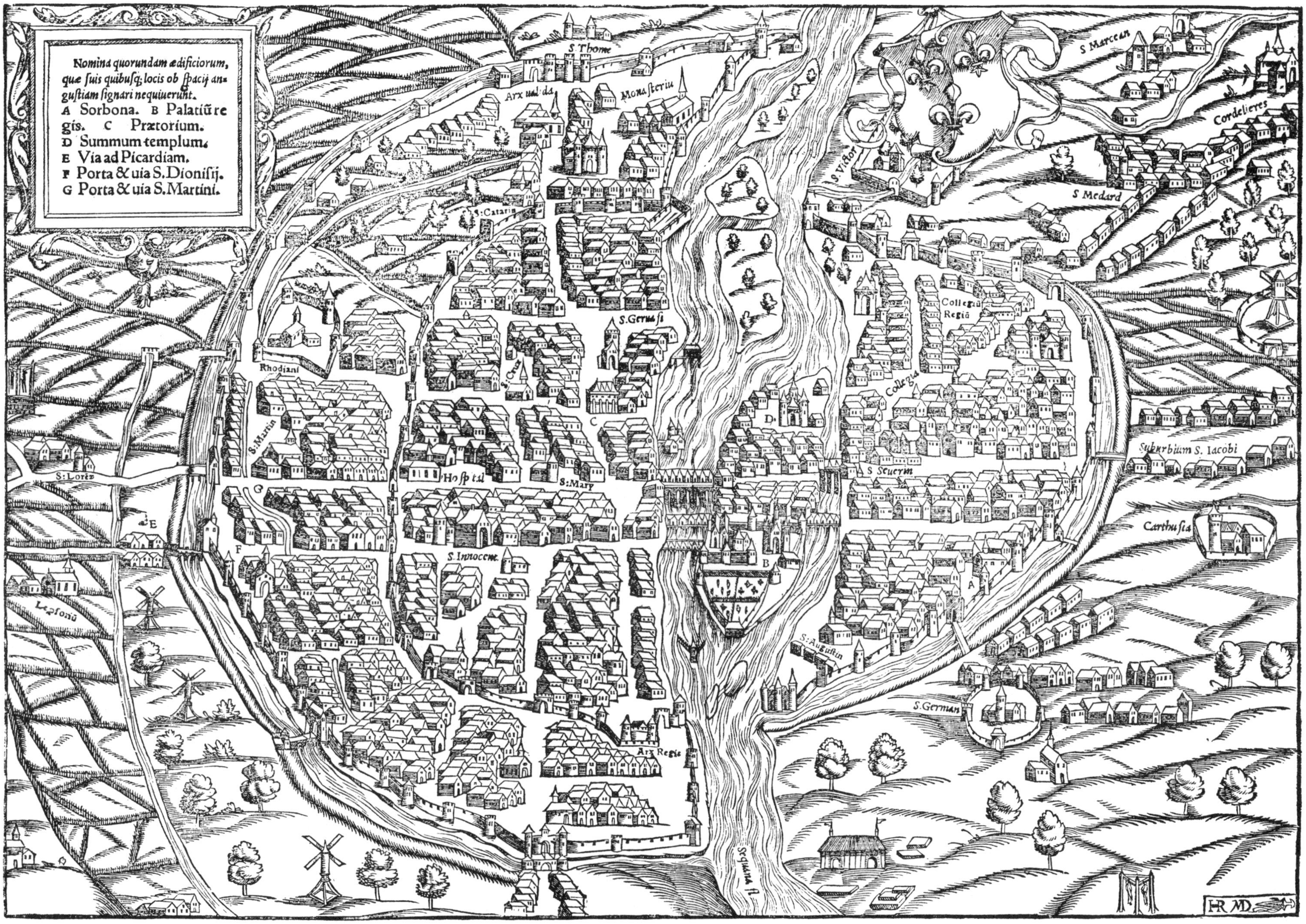

THE CITY OF PARIS.
(SEBASTIAN MUNSTER, "COSMOGRAPHIA UNIVERSALIS," 1550.)

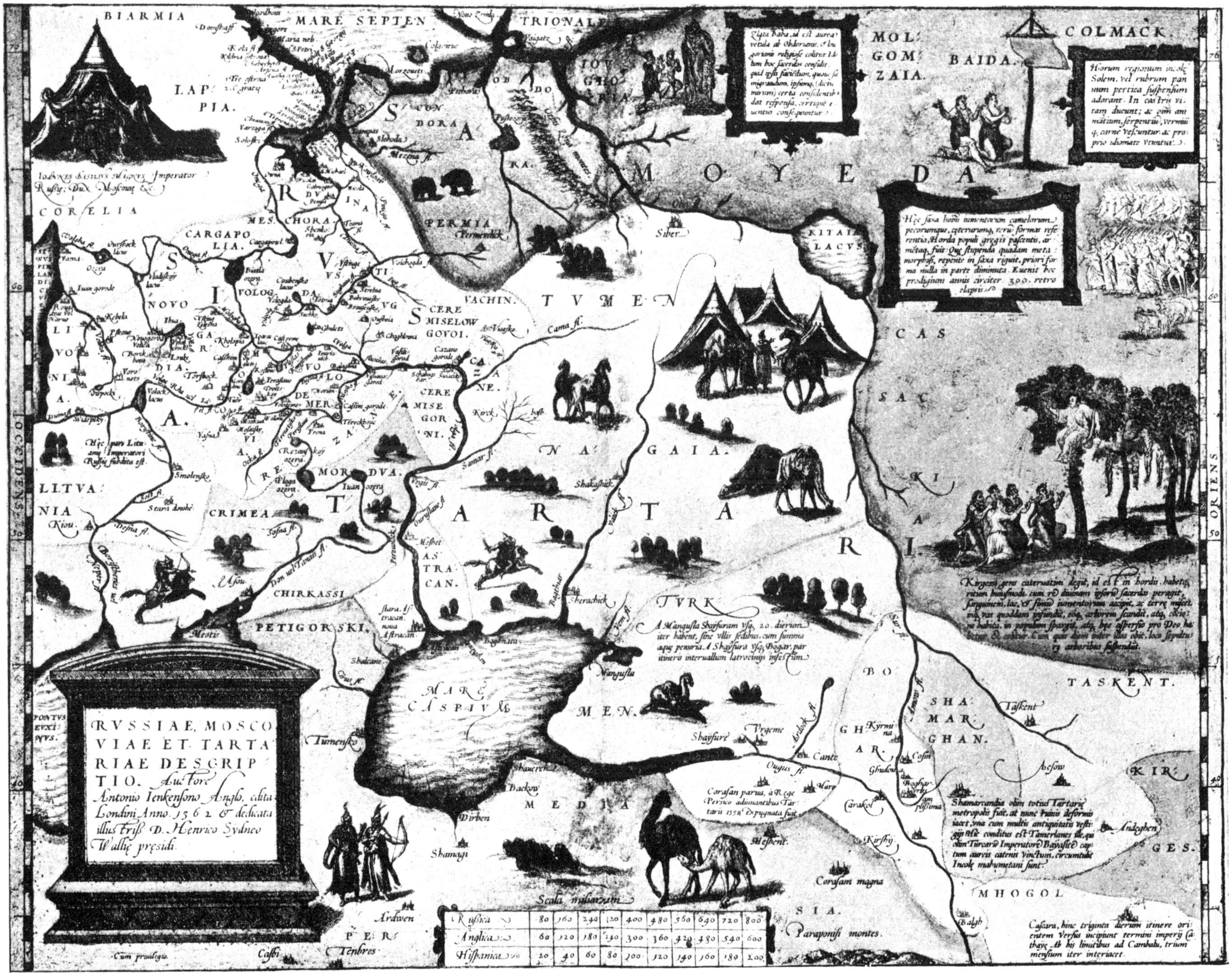

RUSSIA, MUSCOVY AND TARTARY.
(ORTELIUS, "THEATRUM ORBIS TERRARUM," 1570.)

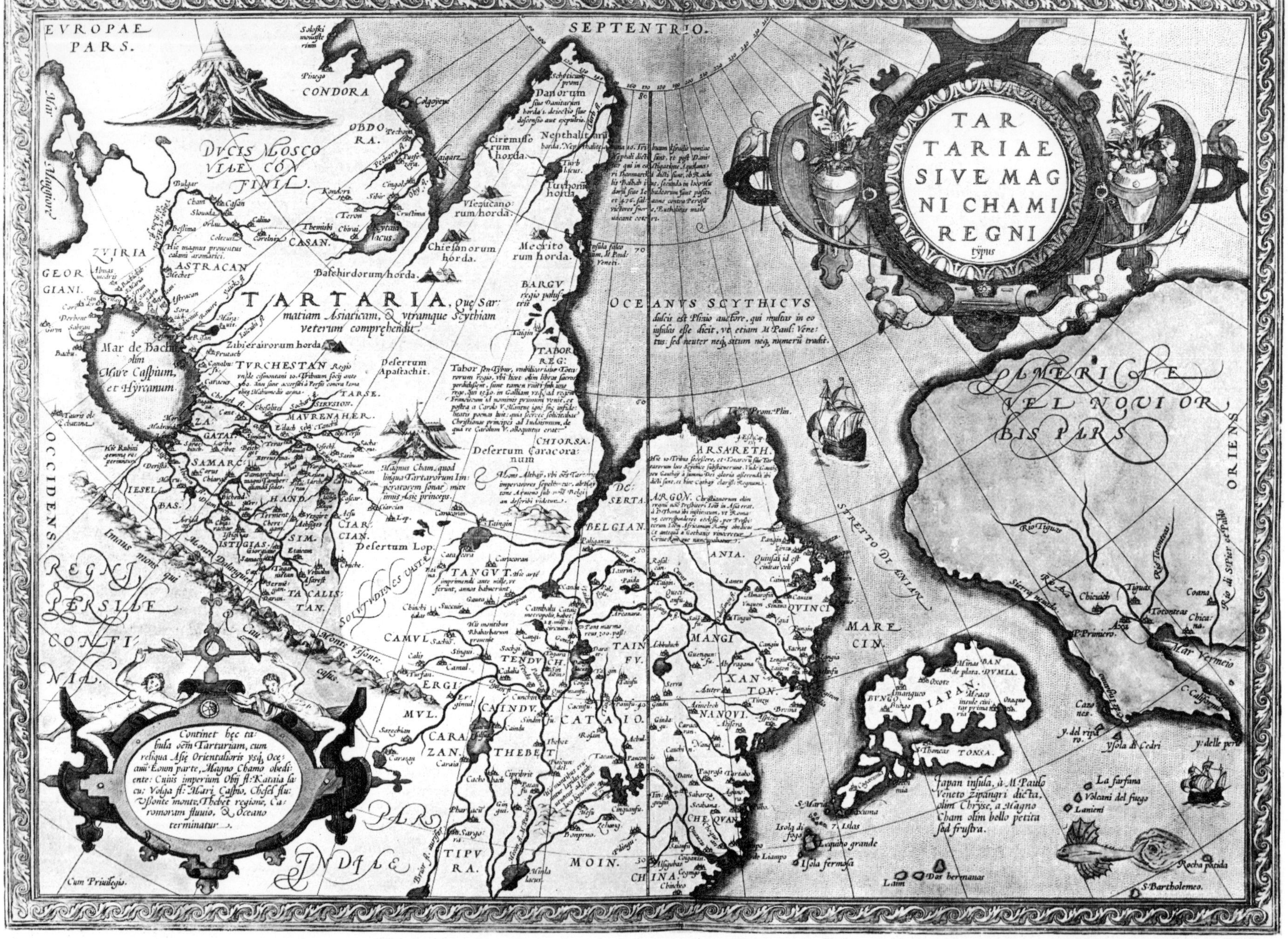

TARTARY, OR THE KINGDOM OF THE GREAT KHAN.
(ORTELIUS, "THEATRUM ORBIS TERRARUM," 1573.)

THE EMPIRE OF PRESTER JOHN, OR ABYSSINIA.
(Ortelius, "Theatrum Orbis Terrarum," 1573.)

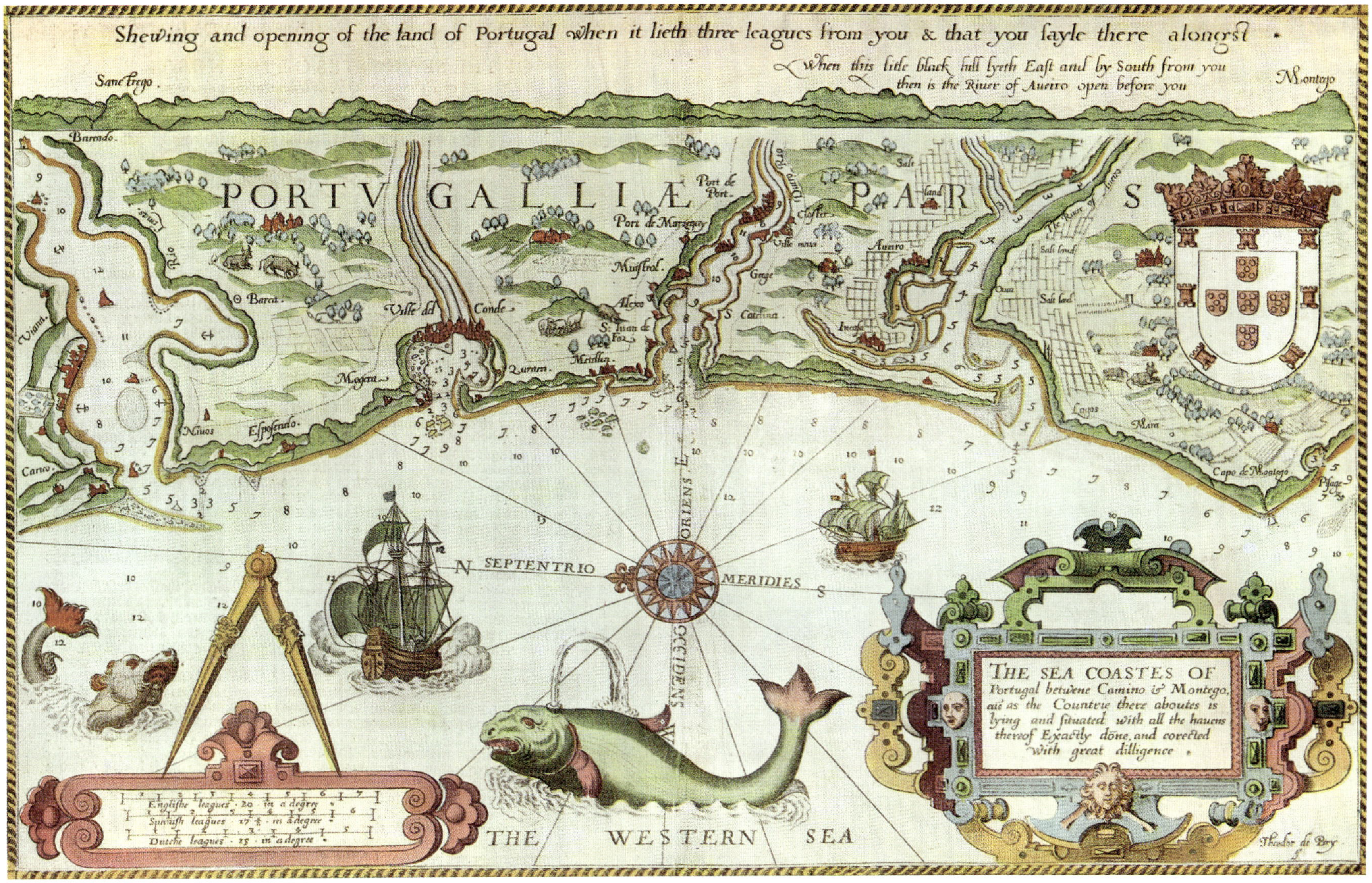

THE NORTHERN COASTAL STRIP OF PORTUGAL, 1588

See previous notes. The Portuguese coats of arms dominate the landmass on which towns, field patterns and hills are identified.

The New World, 1596

Theodore de Bry's map was issued in his volume of voyage reports entitled 'Grands Voyages' and celebrated the voyages of Columbus, Vespucci, Magellan and Pizzaro.

Japan, 1606

A Jodocus Hondius engraving published until 1636 and in 1647 with re-engraved title and decorative features. Korea is shown as an island although the descriptive text states doubt as to whether this is, in fact, correct.

LANCASHIRE, 1611

Engraved, like most of the country maps by Jodocus Hondius this very decorative map features portraits of the rival houses of the Lancastrians and Tudors. Also, typically, the map includes a plan of the city of Lancaster.

Europe, 1619-1672

Guillaume Blaeu's fine series of maps of the continents were first issued separately around the 1620s and appeared, in atlas form, from 1630 in the Atlantis Appendix. The style now termed 'cartes à figures' was popularly practised by Dutch and English map-makers during the seventeenth century and usually, as here, had figured side borders and, above, plans or panoramas of that area's major cities. The Blaeu family, until about 1670, were responsible for some of the finest map production of the time – their work culminating in 1662 with the publication of the Atlas Major, some 600-plus maps of all parts of the world bound together in eleven or twelve uniform atlas volumes invariably of vellum or the finest morocco leather. Finely engraved, often found in colour applied at the time by the Blaeu publishing house these are amongst the most sought-after maps by collectors today.

Throughout their long periods of usage – in the case of this map from 1619 to 1672 – few of the maps had any engraved updating. This is one of the few where alterations were made. The original map included the mythical island of Frisland to the south-west of Iceland and this was removed from the copperplate about 1660.

Africa, c 1619-1672

See previous note. Blaeu's fine maps of the continent incorporates numerous animals, birds and fish to illustrate the fauna of this land mass where coastlines were well known to Europeans but whose interior was very much a matter for conjecture.

THE WORLD, 1627

John Speed's World map was not only the first map in the first world atlas produced by an Englishman but is also one of the earliest to be found which shows the cartographical misconception which lasted virtually one hundred years – that of California being shown as an island.

Decorating the map's borders are representations of the four elements – earth, fire, air and water; portraits of explorers and astronomical diagrams.

The World, 1630

Henricus Hondius' World map was used in the sequence of atlases, described above, and was one of the most up-to-date of the period. Of particular interest is detail in the Gulf or Carpentaria – on Australia's north coast based on Dutch landings in 1616. Not dissimilar to John Speed's map this is more finely engraved and has portraits of Caesar, Ptolemy, Mercator and Jodocus Hondius – the author's father.

THE HOLY LAND.
(Ortelius, "Theatrum Orbis Terrarum.")

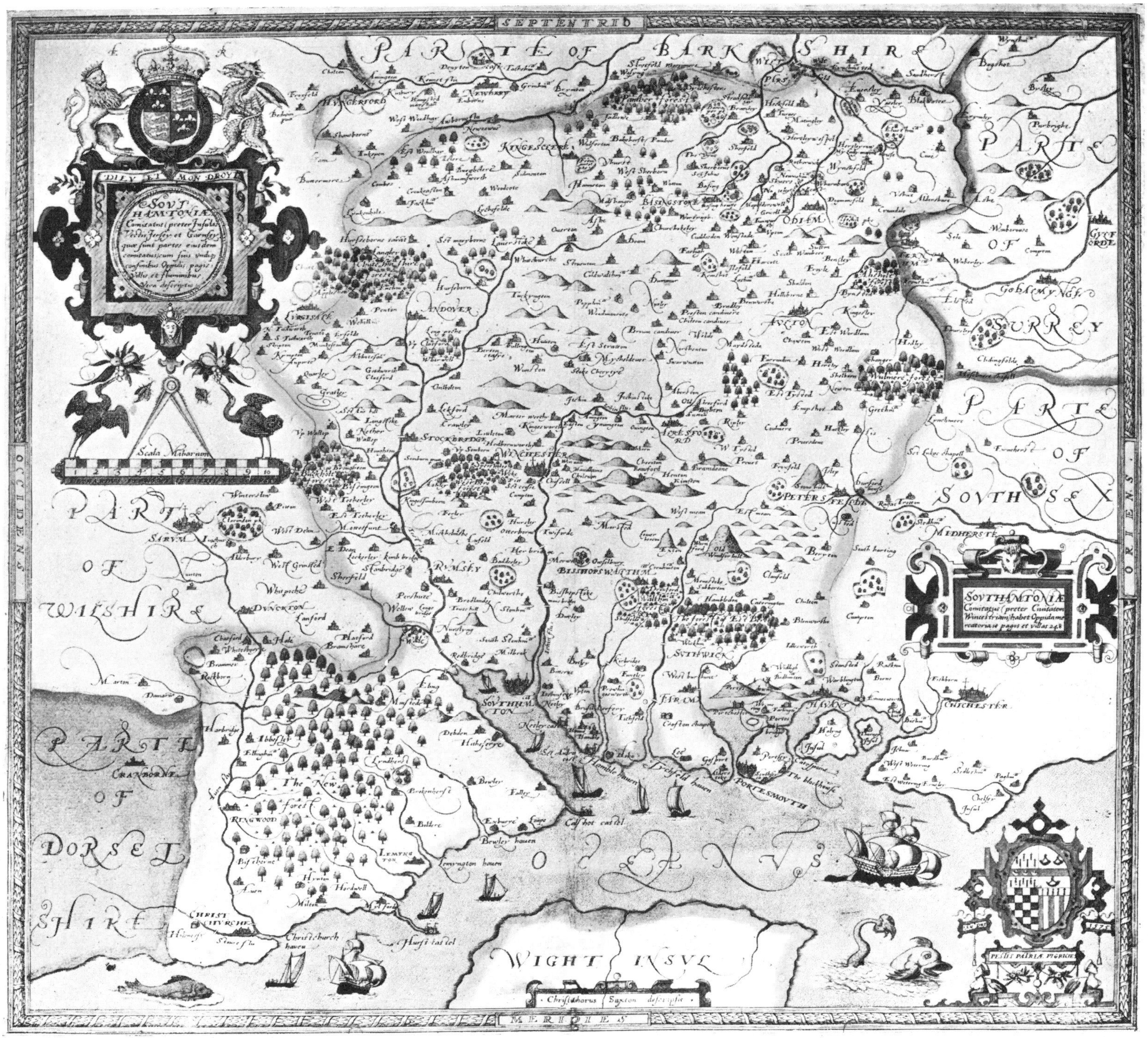

THE COUNTY OF SOUTHAMPTON.
(SAXTON'S ATLAS OF THE COUNTIES OF ENGLAND, 1574-9.)

ASIA EAST OF THE GANGES.
(Ptolemy, "Geographia," *Cologne*, 1584.)

TITLE PAGE TO
WAGENAR, "THE MARINER'S MIRROR," 1588.

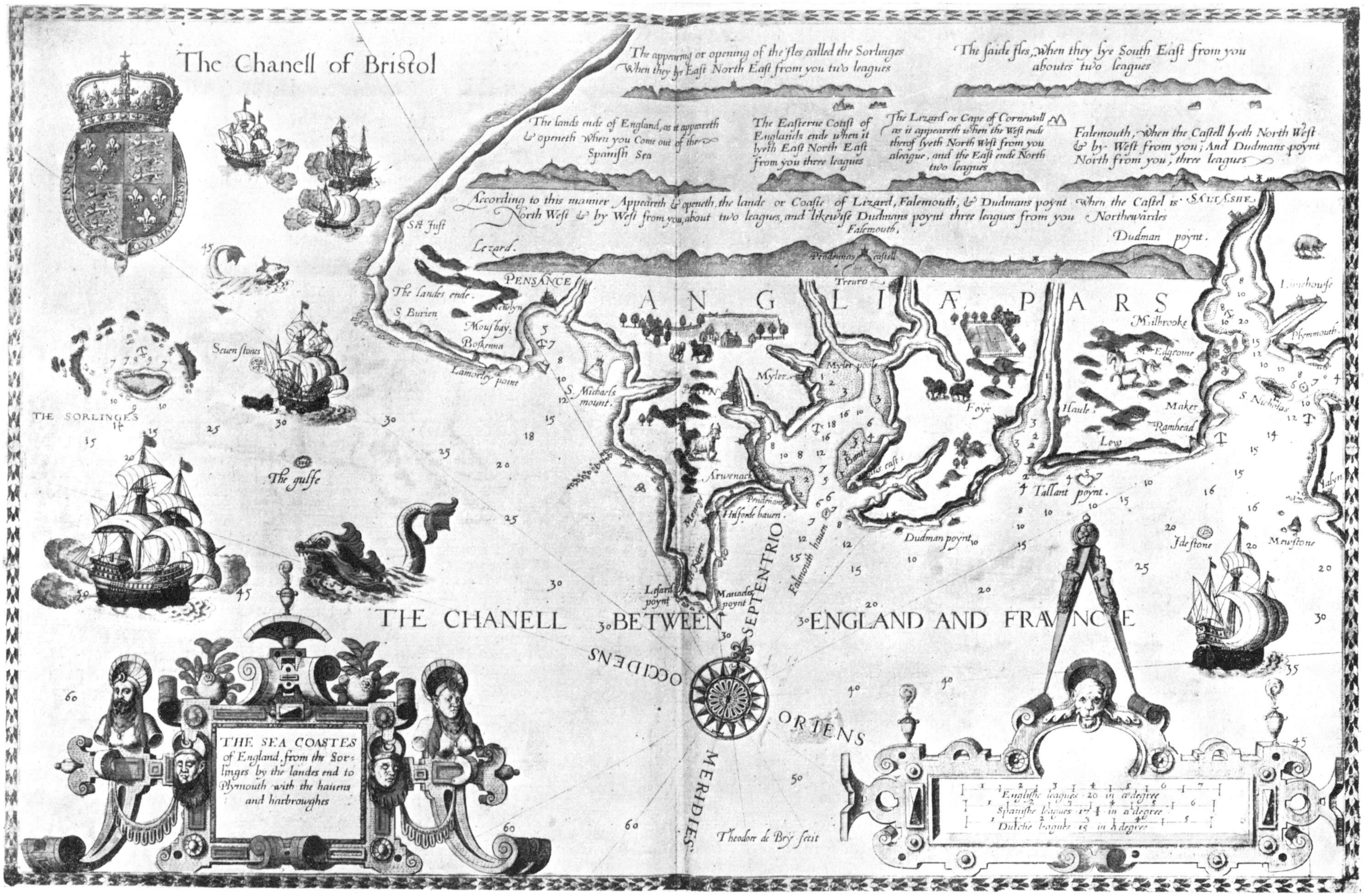

THE SEA COASTS OF ENGLAND FROM THE SORLINGES (SCILLIES) BY LAND'S END TO PLYMOUTH.
(WAGENAR, "THE MARINER'S MIRROR," 1588.)

CONSTANTINOPLE.
(Braun & Hogenberg, "Civitates Orbis Terrarum," 1574-1618; Book I.)

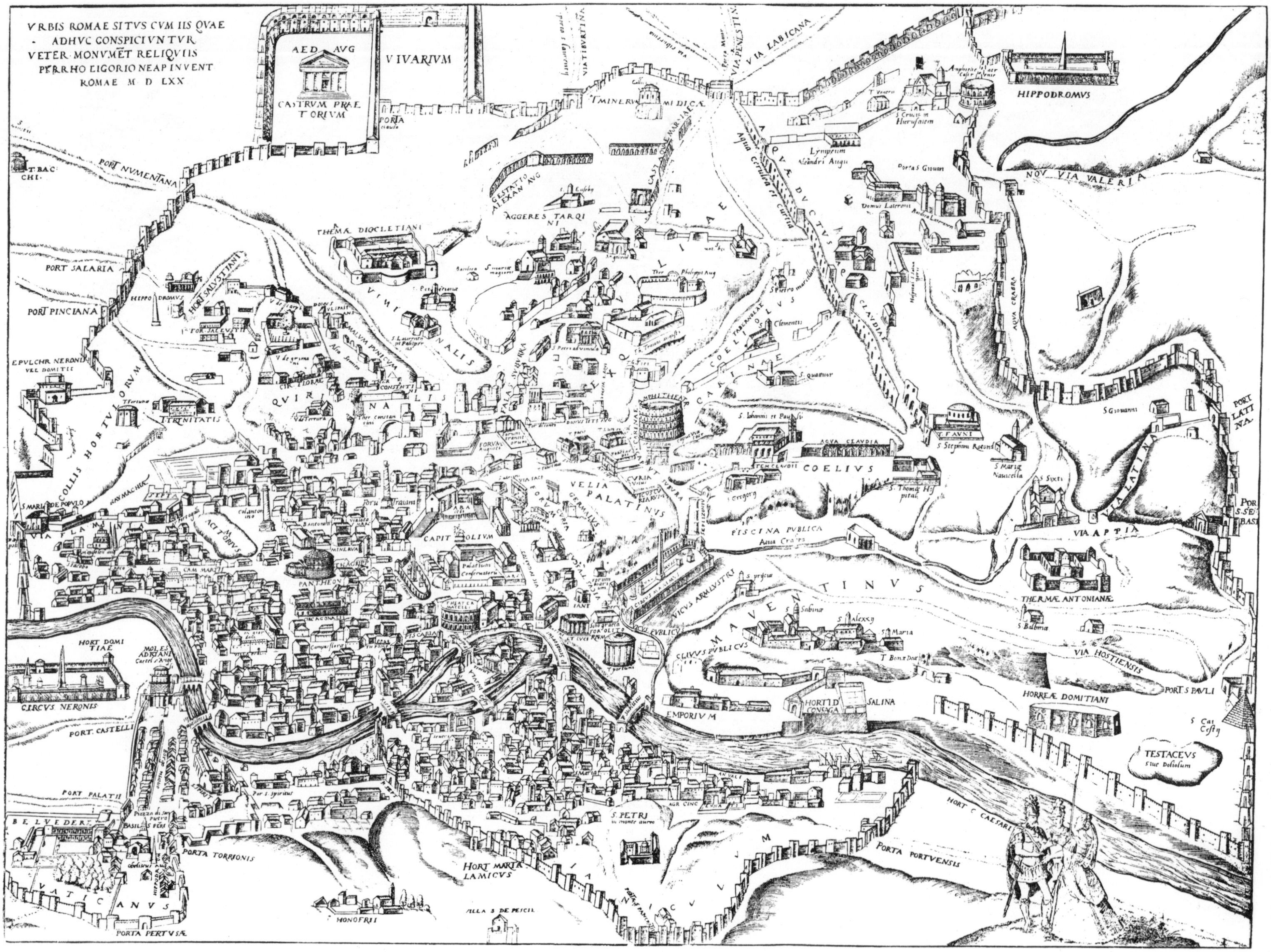

THE CITY OF ROME WITH ITS ANCIENT MONUMENTS.
(BRAUN & HOGENBERG, "CIVITATES CREIS TERRARUM," 1574-1618; BOOK II.)

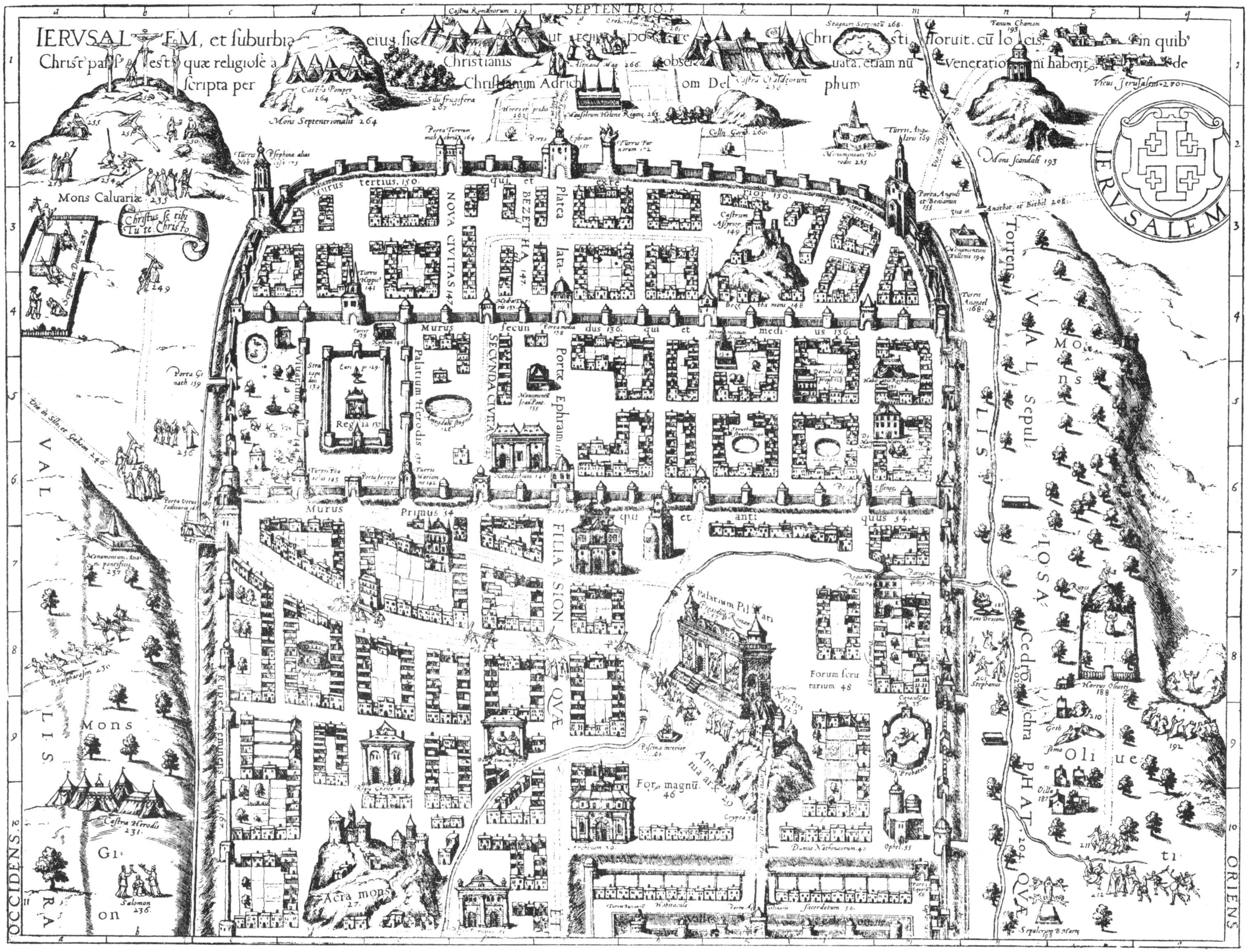

JERUSALEM AND ITS SUBURBS.
(Braun & Hogenberg, "Civitates Orbis Terrarum," 1574-1618; Book IV.)

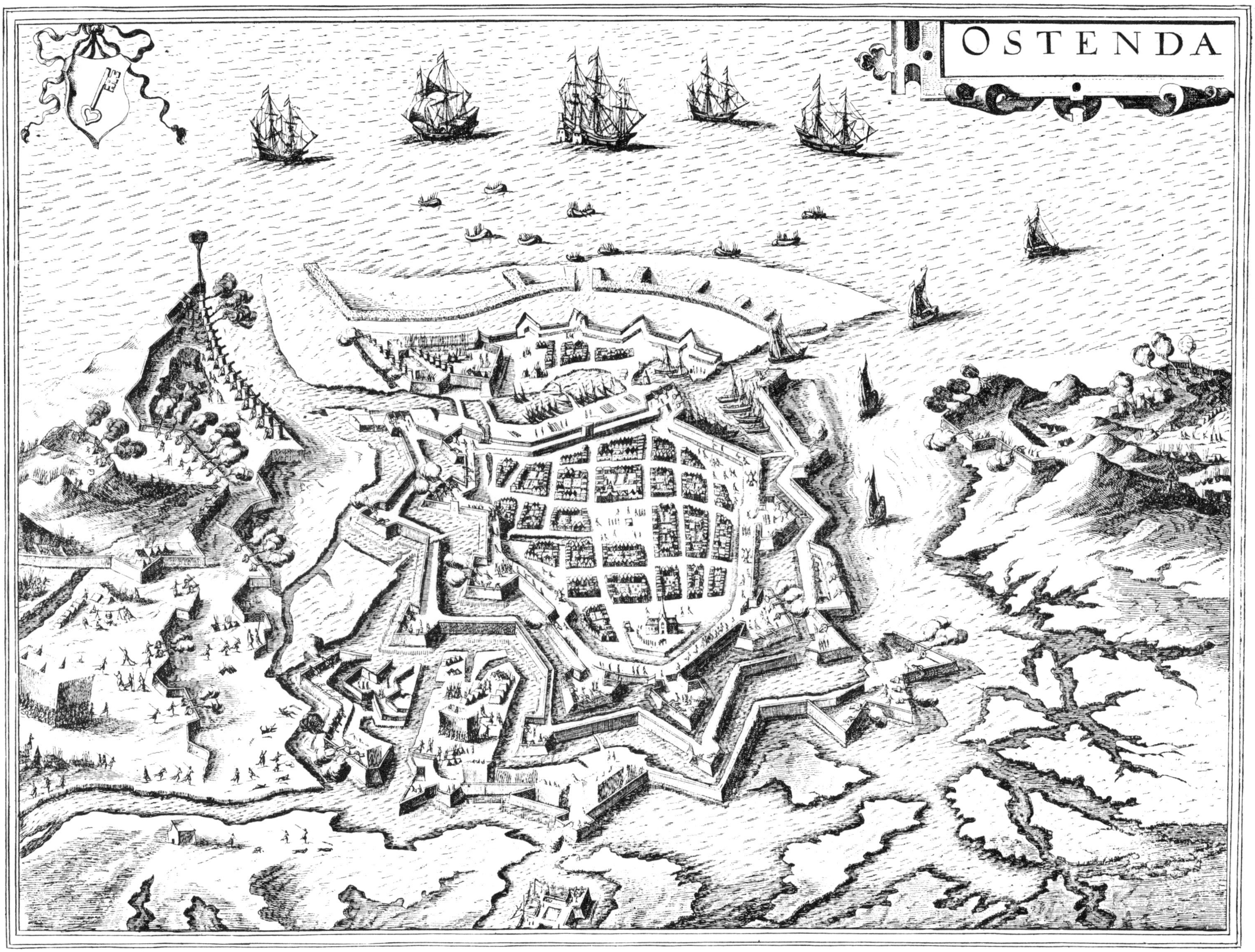

OSTEND (DURING THE SIEGE OF 1601-4?).
(BRAUN & HOGENBERG, "CIVITATES ORBIS TERRARUM," 1574-1618; BOOK VI.)

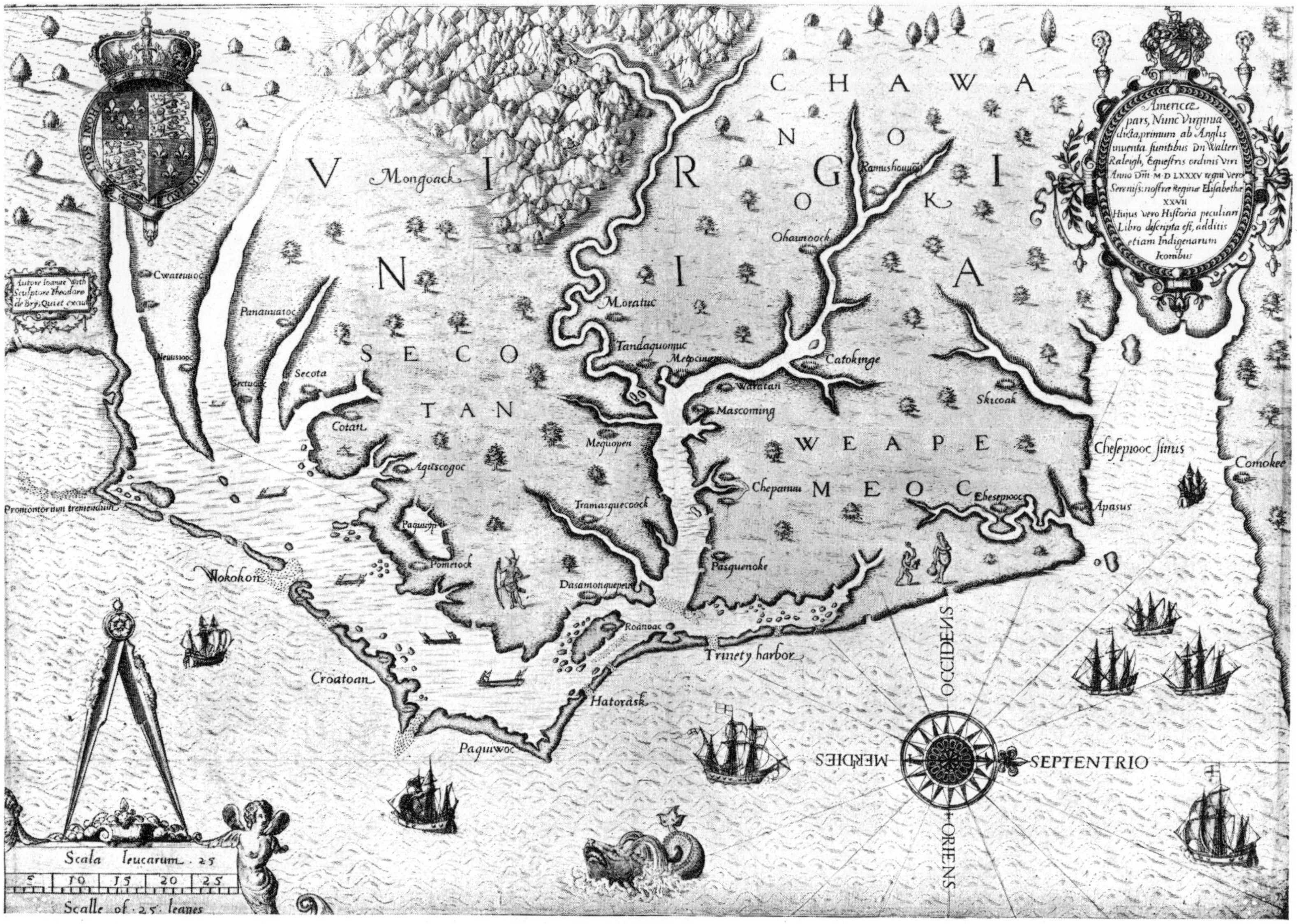

VIRGINIA.
(De Bry, Grand Voyages, Part I., *Frankfort*, 1590.)
(*Macpherson Collection, Naval Section.*)

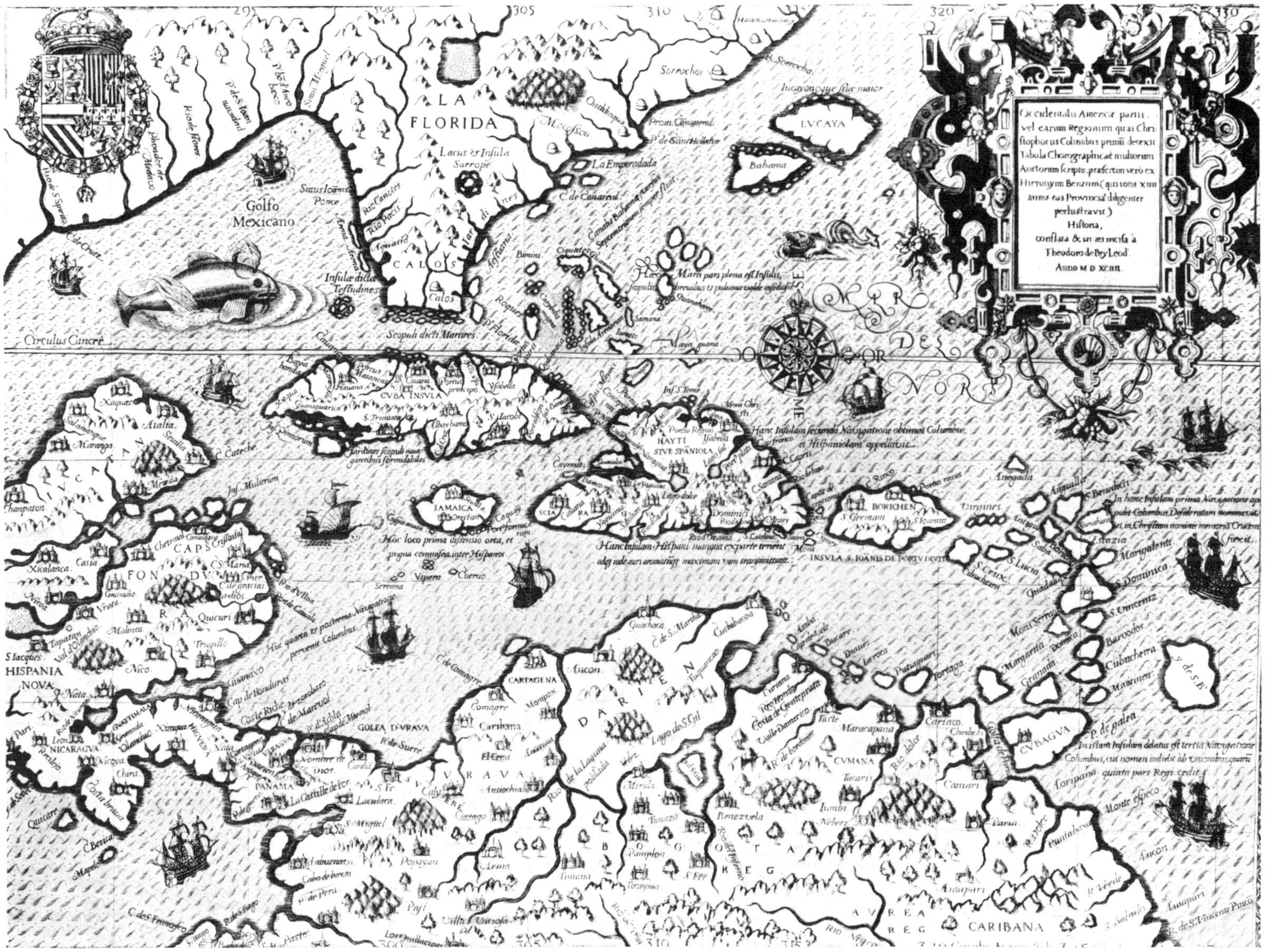

CENTRAL AMERICA (HERE CALLED AMERICA OCCIDENTALIS.)
(DE BRY, GRAND VOYAGES, PART IV., *Frankfort,* 1594.)
(*Macpherson Collection, Naval Section.*)

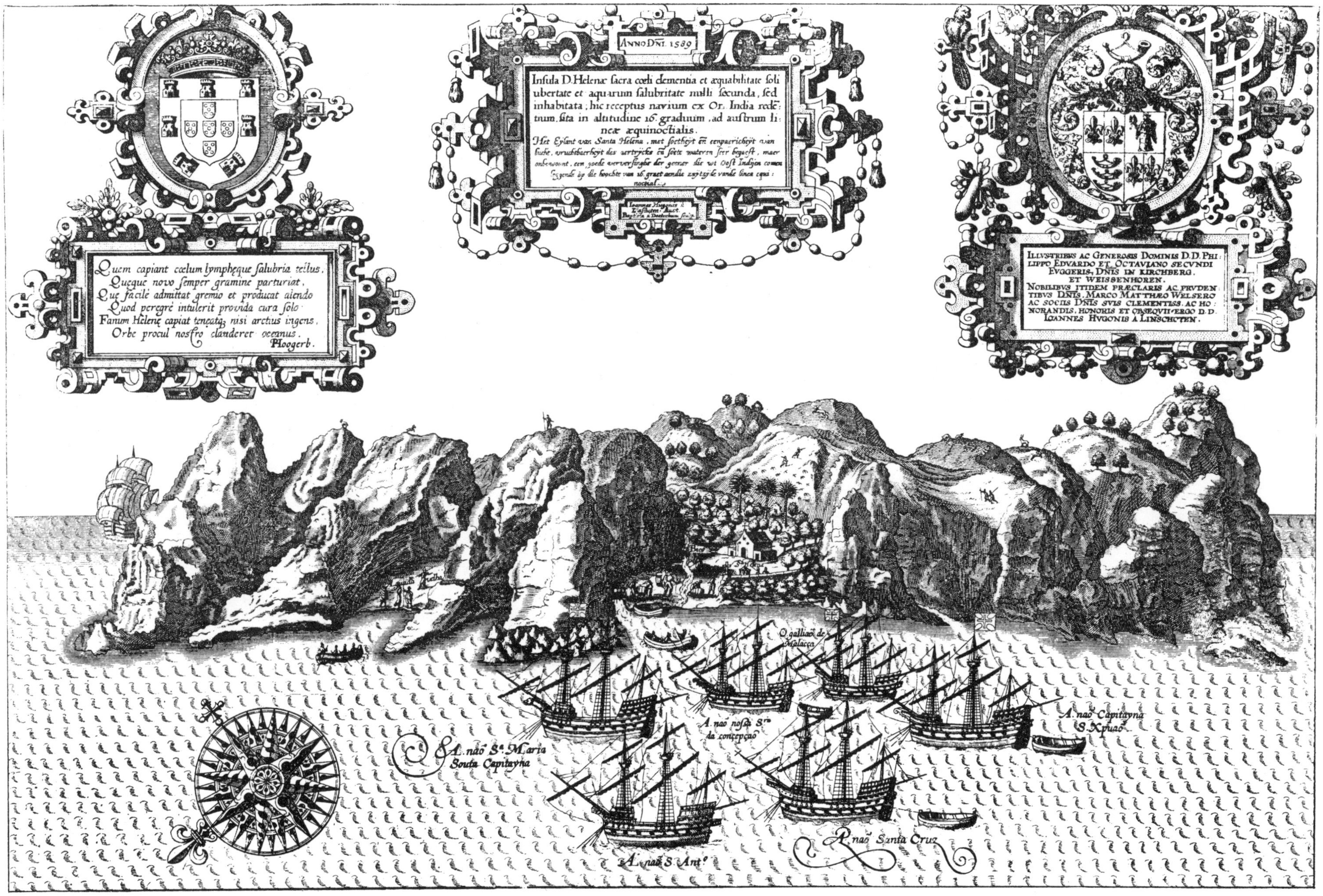

THE ISLAND OF ST. HELENA.
(LINSCHOTEN, "NAVIGATIO AC ITINERARIUM, ETC.", 1599.)

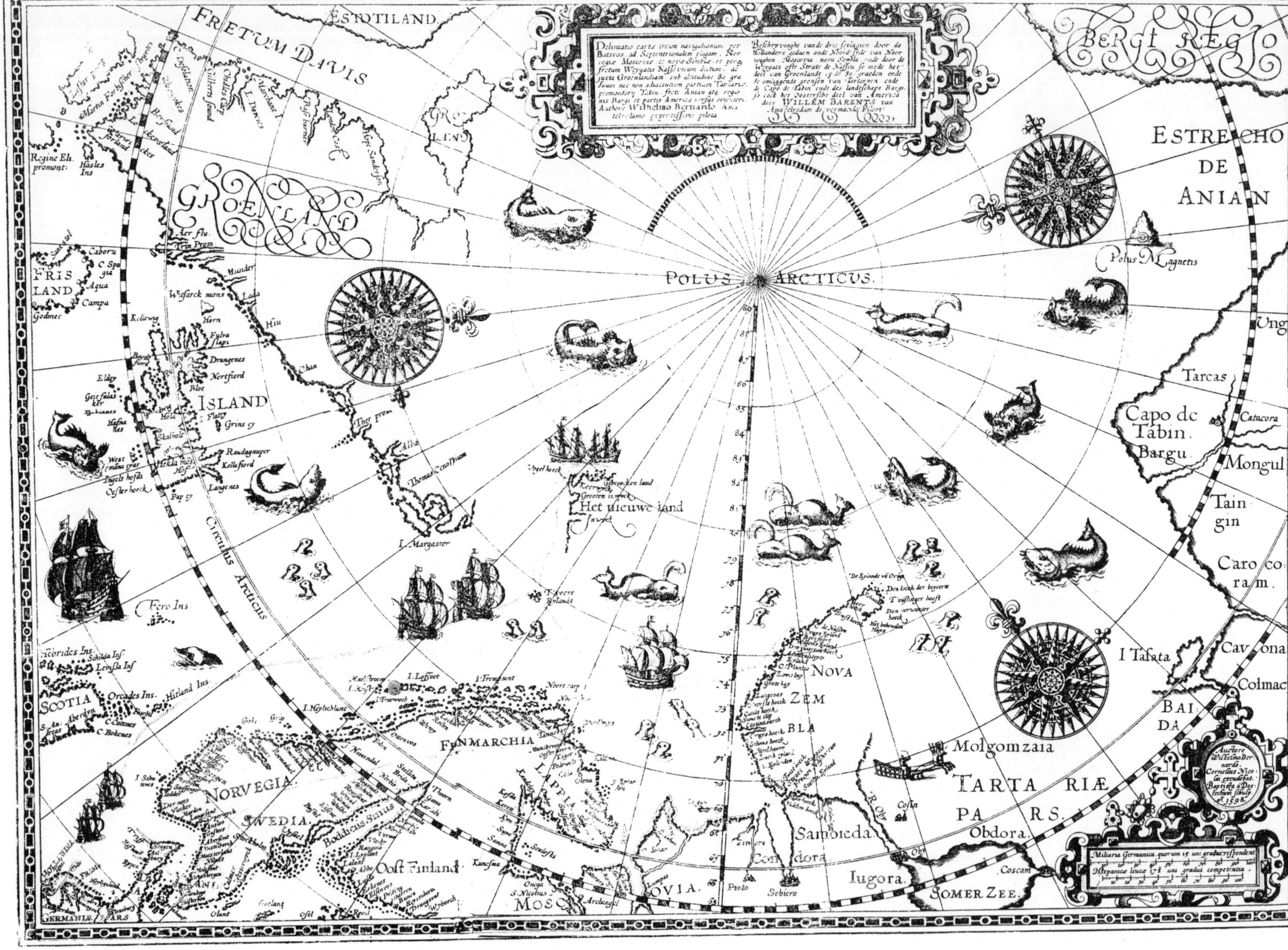

THE NORTH POLAR REGIONS.
(LINSCHOTEN, "NAVIGATIO AC ITINERARIUM, ETC.", 1599.)

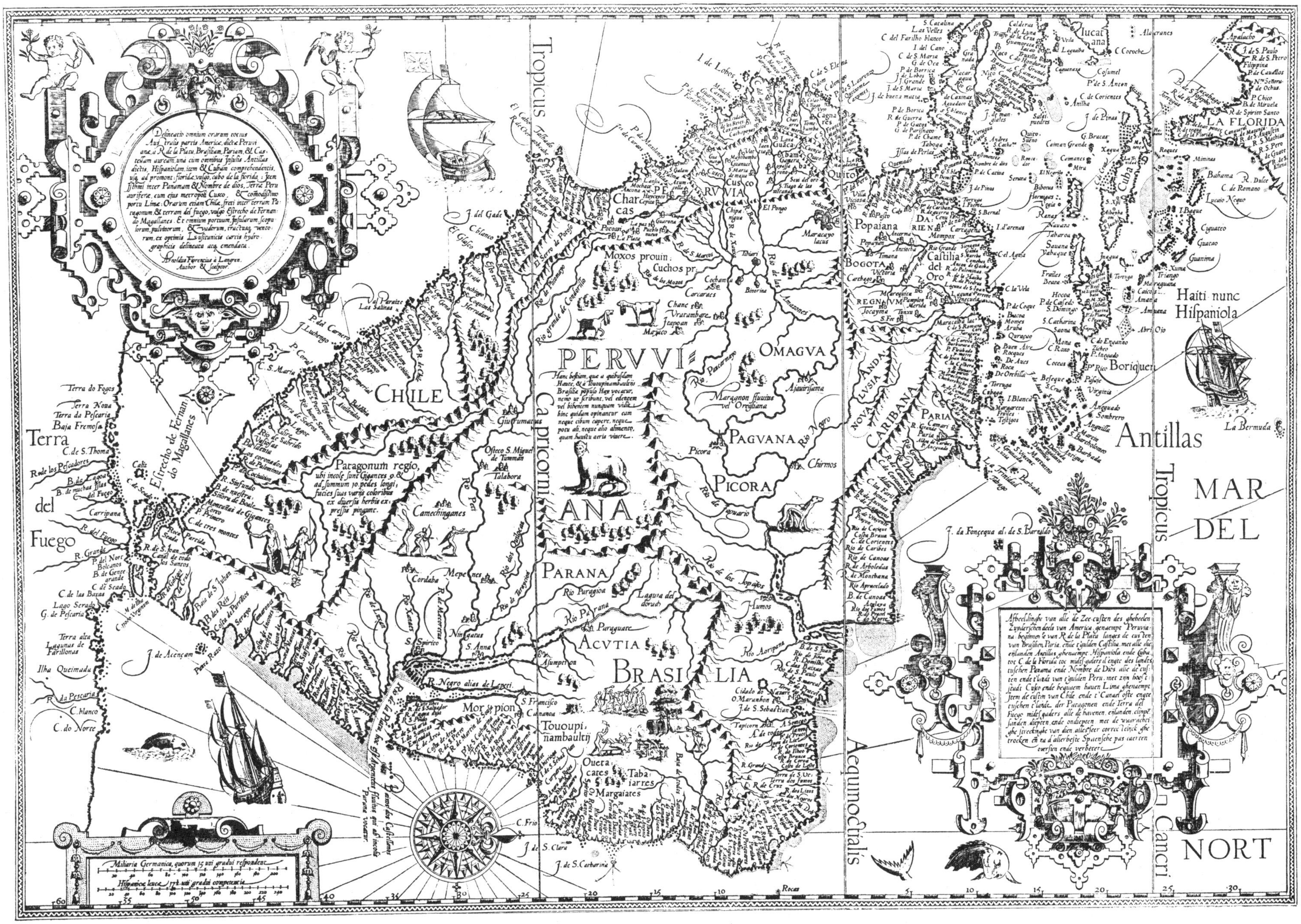

THE SEA COASTS OF SOUTH AMERICA.
(LINSCHOTEN, "NAVIGATIO AC ITINERARIUM, ETC.", 1599.)

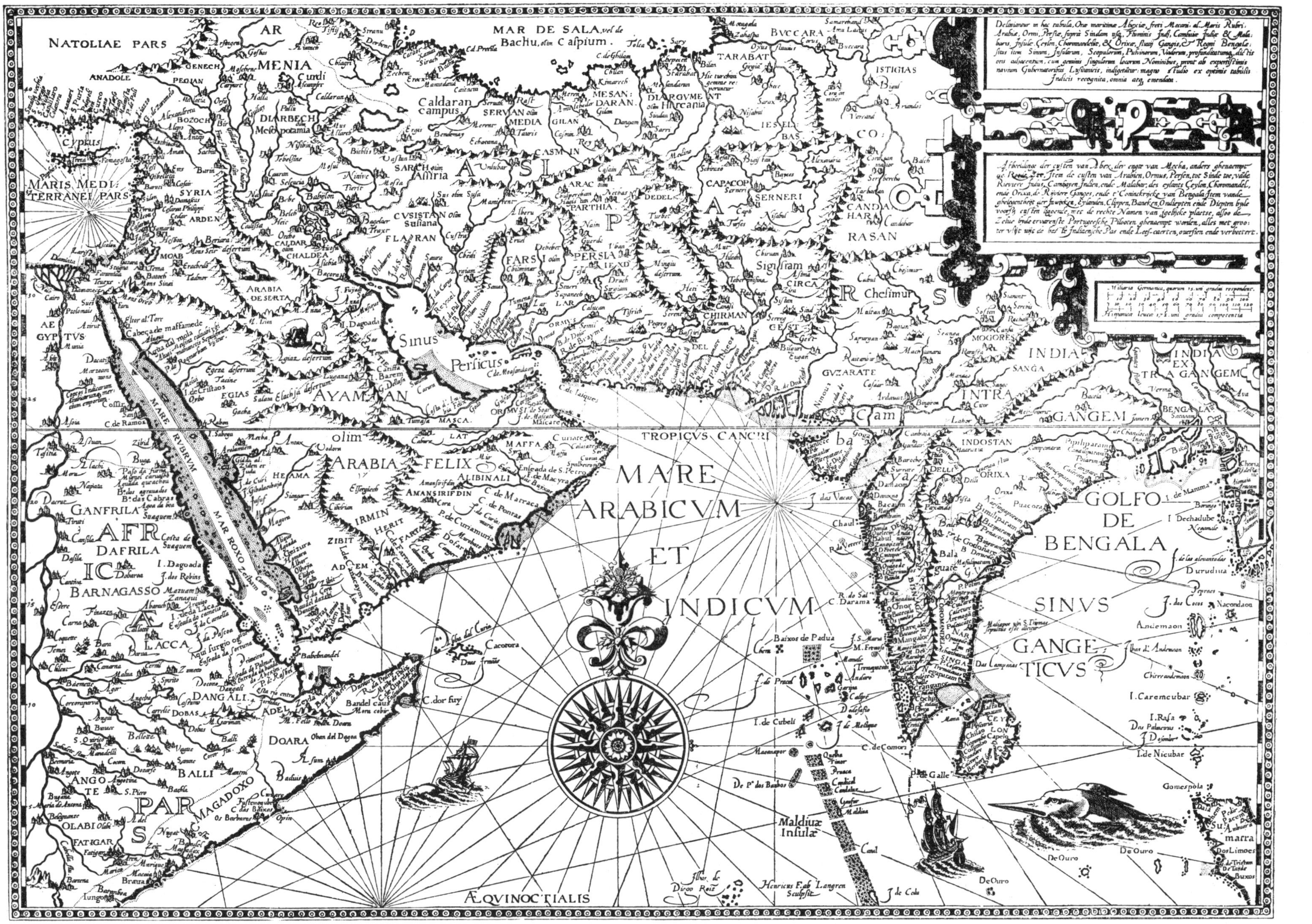

NORTH-EAST AFRICA, ARABIA, PERSIA, AND INDIA.
(LINSCHOTEN, "NAVIGATIO AC ITINERARIUM, ETC.", 1599.)

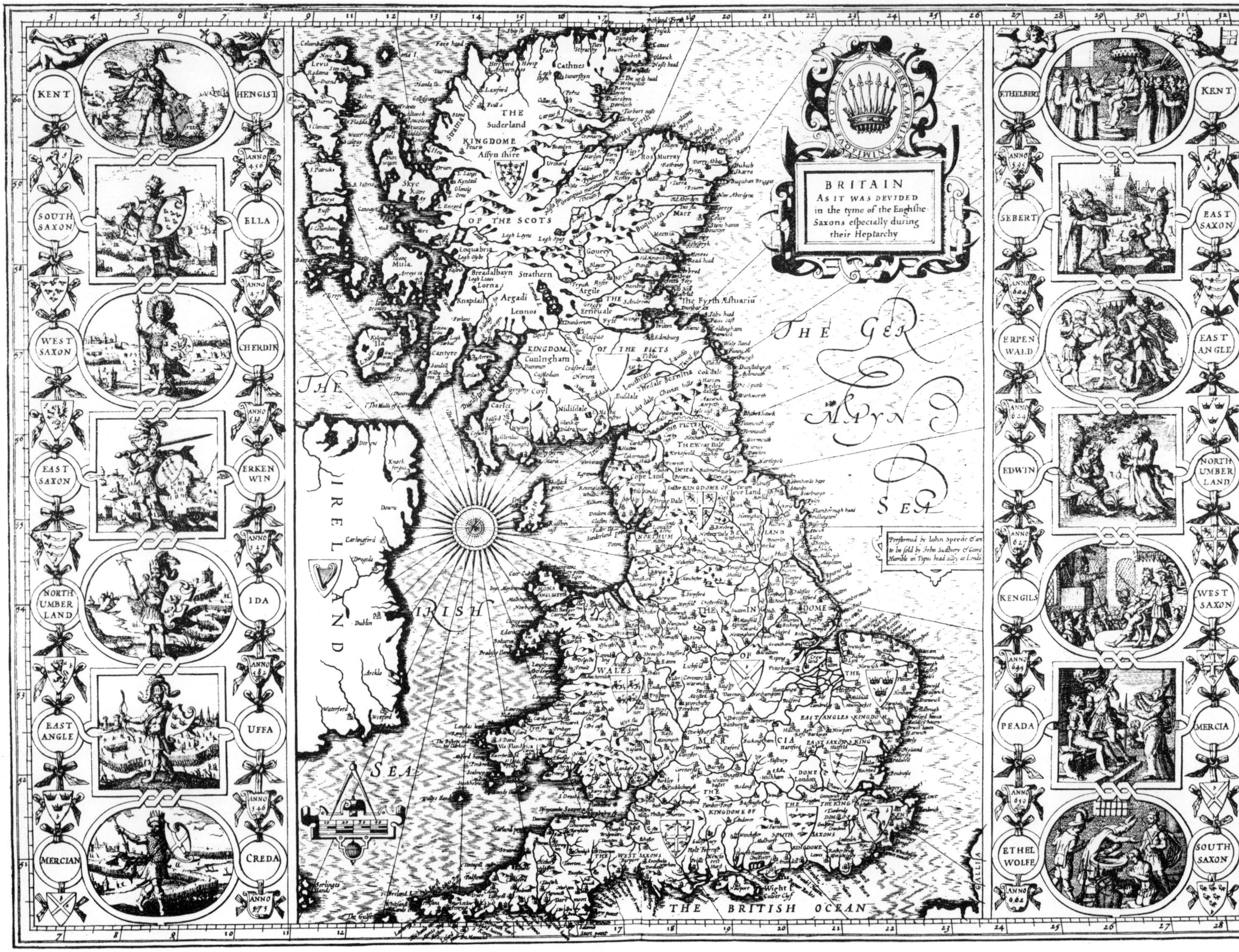

BRITAIN AT THE TIME OF THE SAXON HEPTARCHY.
(SPEED, "THE THEATRE OF THE EMPIRE OF GREAT BRITAIN," 1611.)

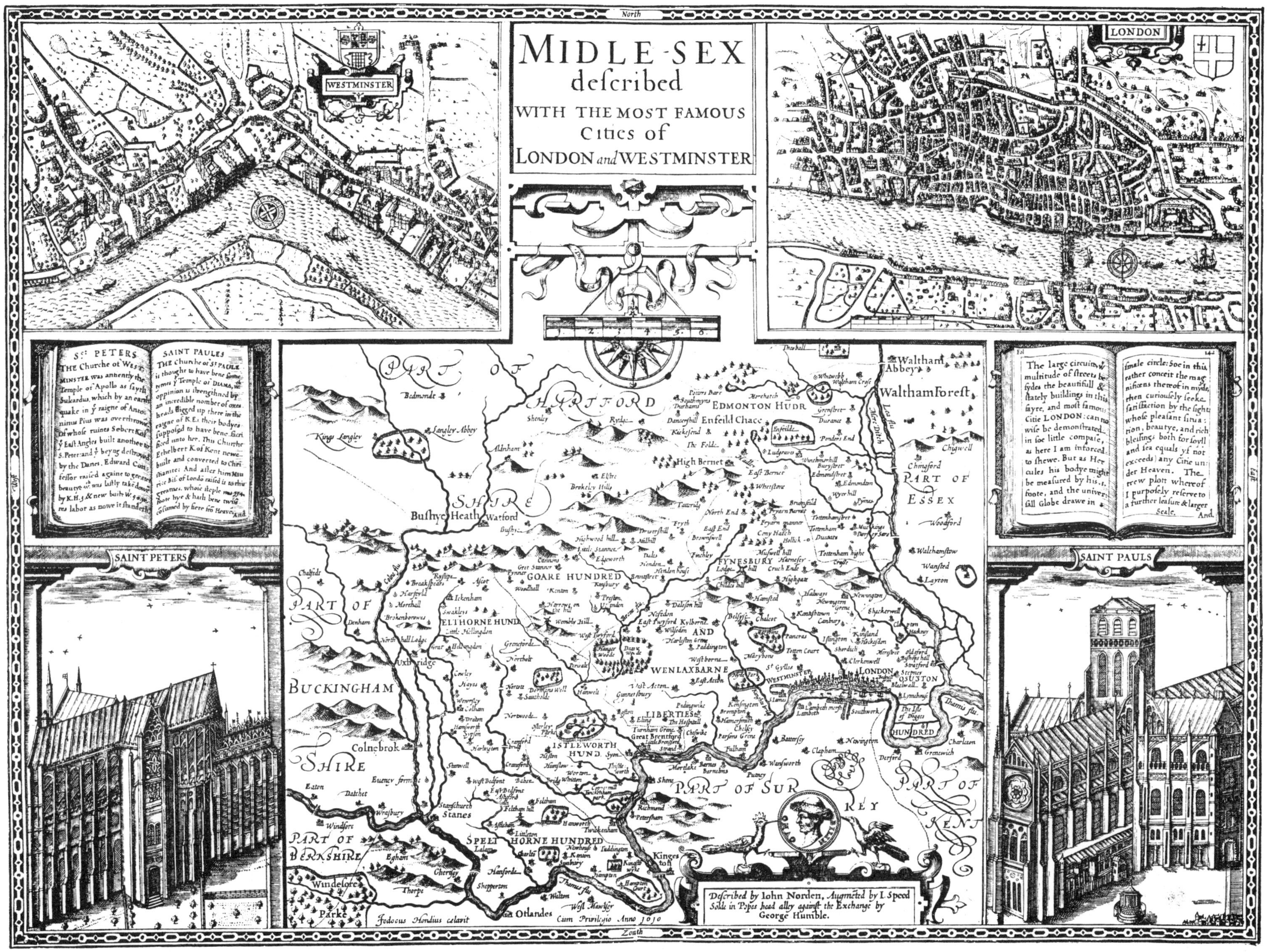

MIDDLESEX, WITH THE CITIES OF LONDON AND WESTMINSTER.
(SPEED, "THE THEATRE OF THE EMPIRE OF GREAT BRITAIN," 1611.)

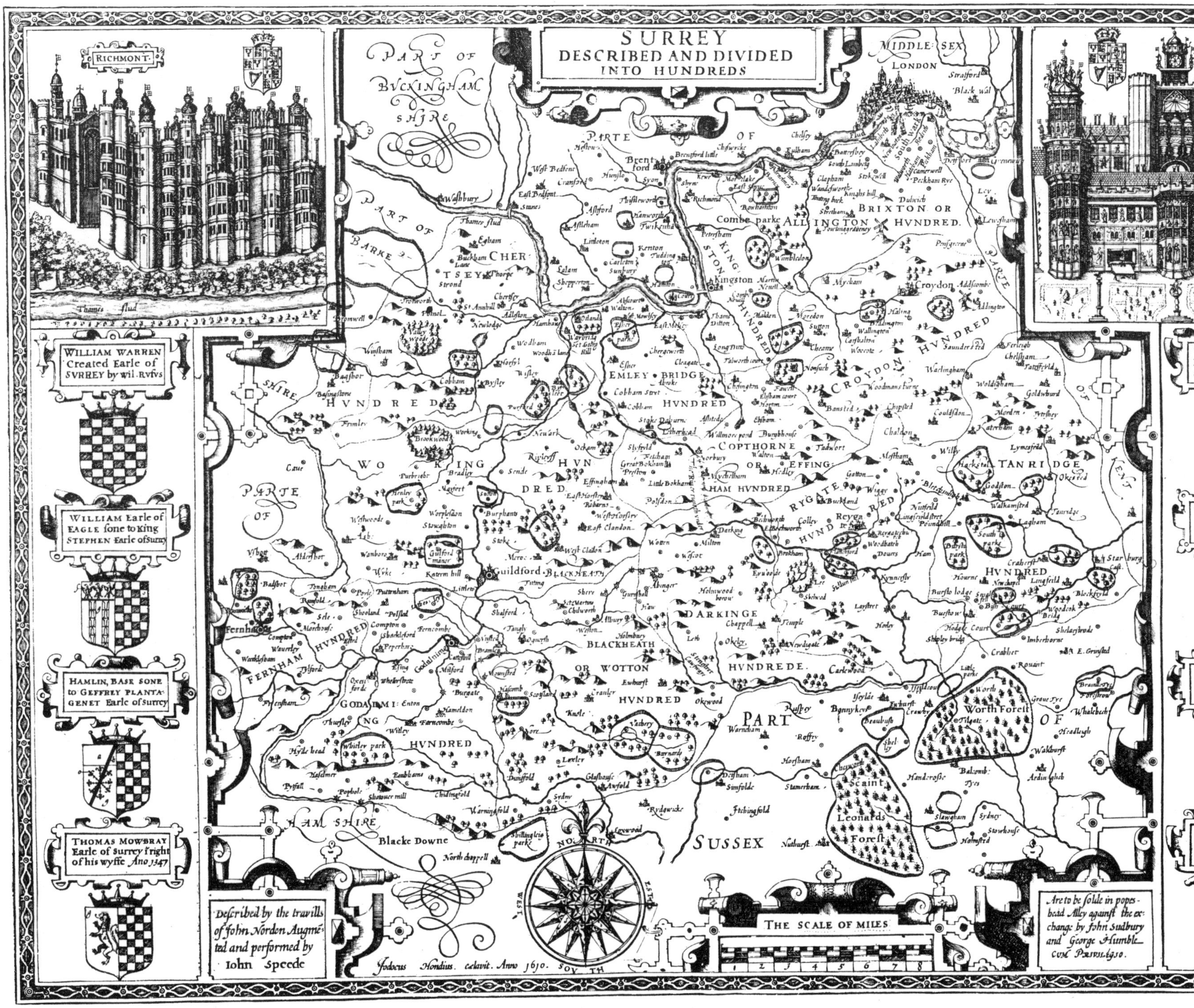

THE COUNTY OF SURREY.

(SPEED, "THE THEATRE OF THE EMPIRE OF GREAT BRITAIN," 1611.)

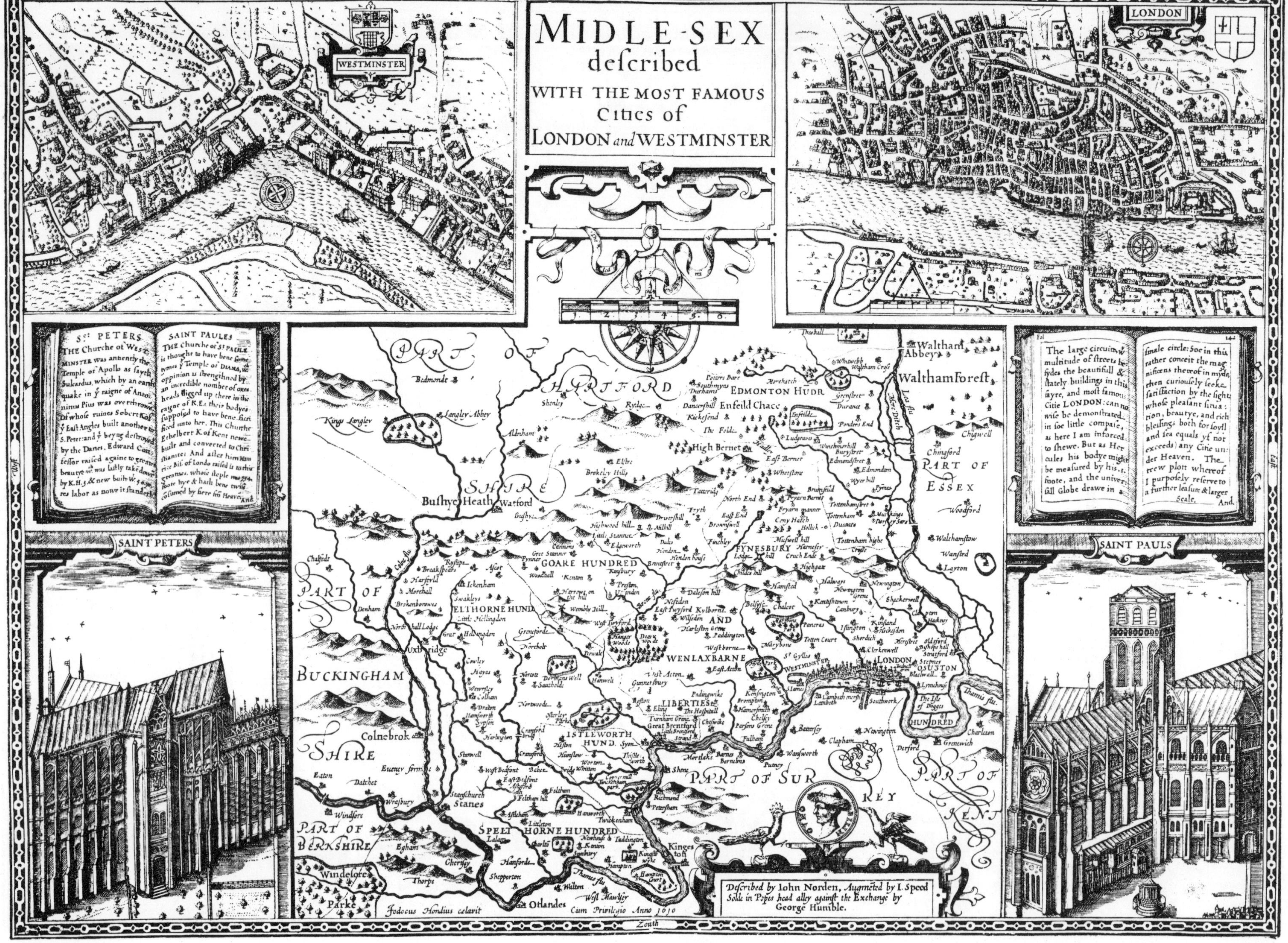

MIDDLESEX, WITH THE CITIES OF LONDON AND WESTMINSTER.
(SPEED, "THE THEATRE OF THE EMPIRE OF GREAT BRITAIN," 1611.)

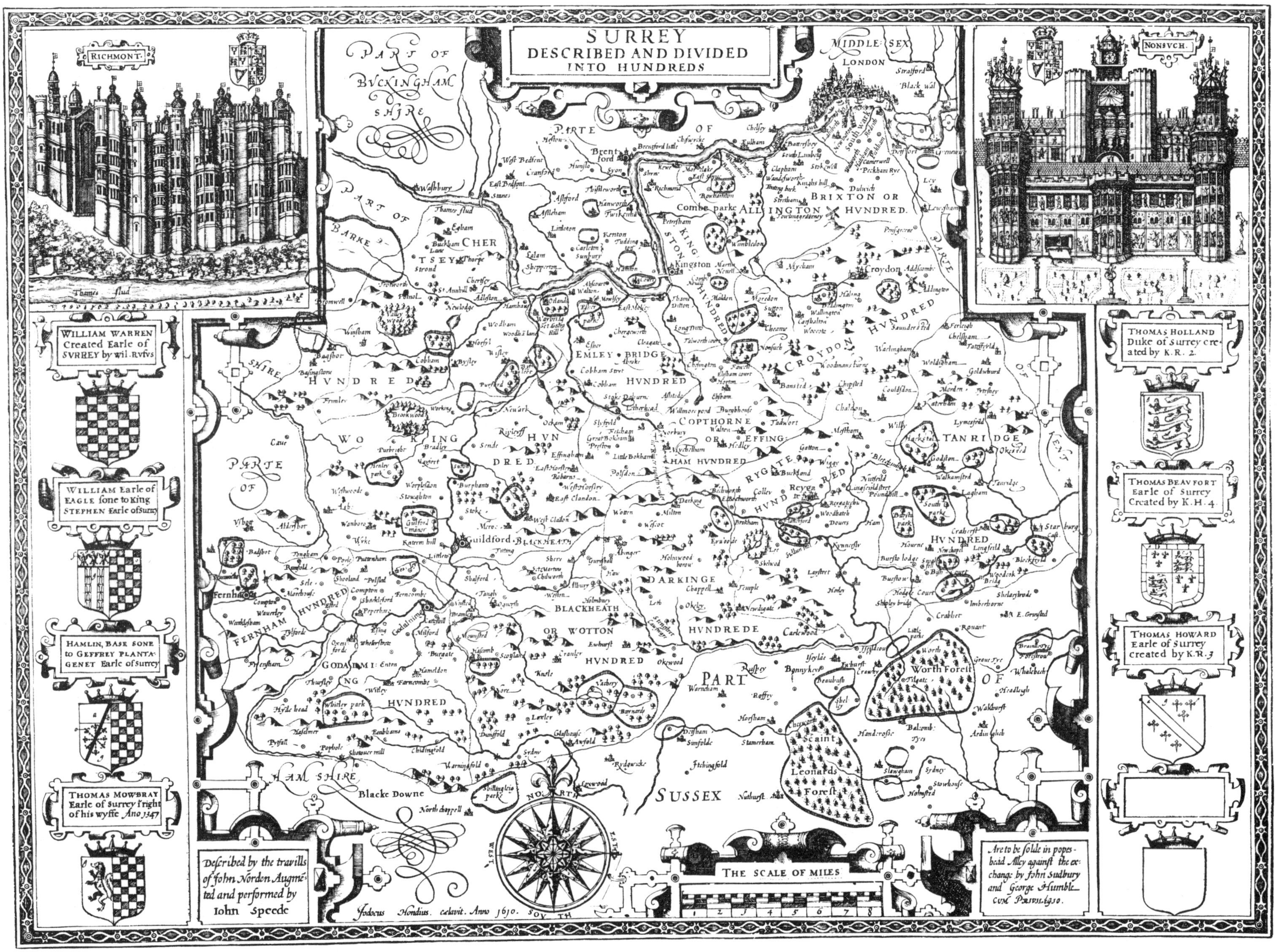

THE COUNTY OF SURREY.
(SPEED, "THE THEATRE OF THE EMPIRE OF GREAT BRITAIN," 1611.)

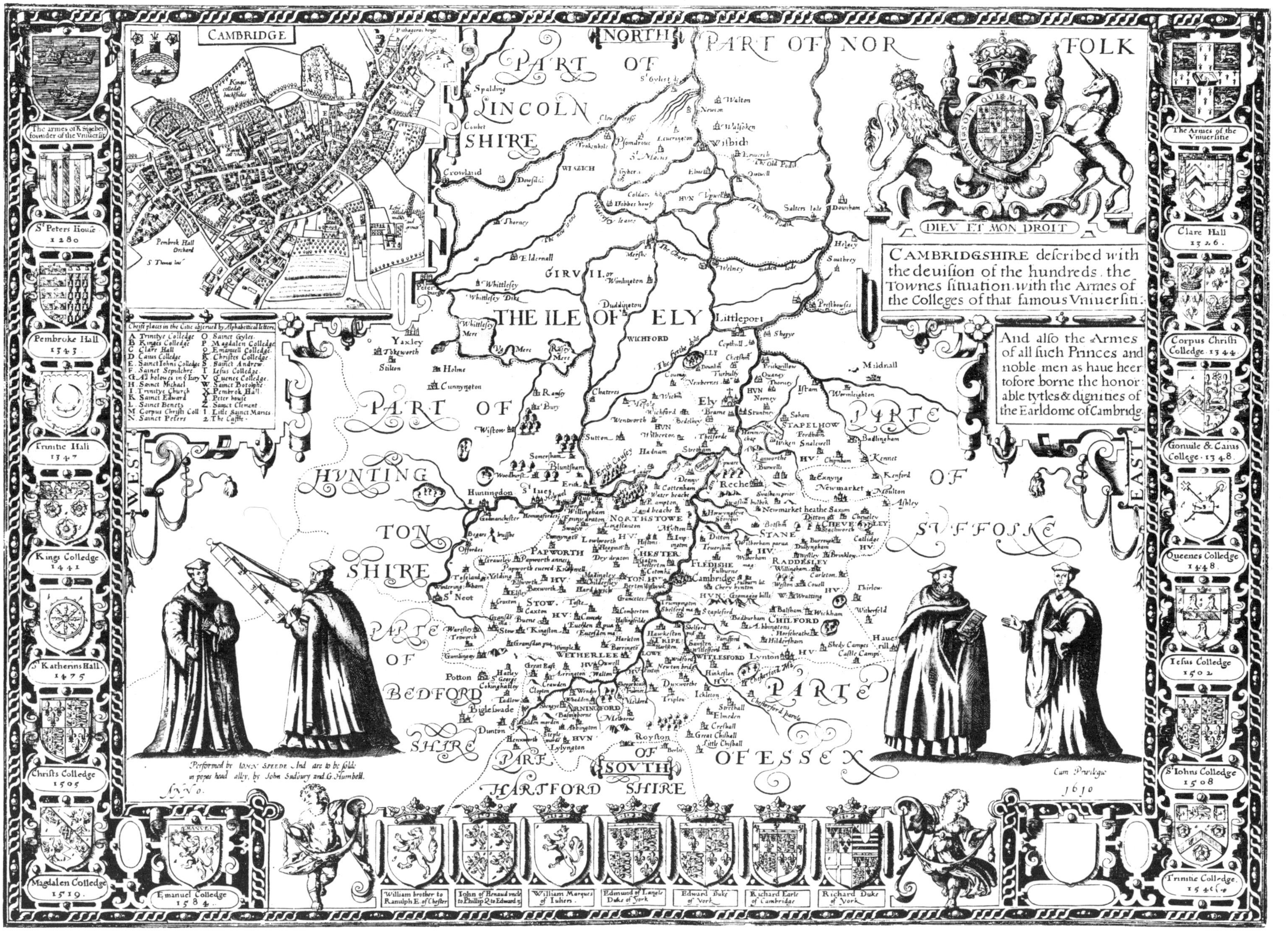

CAMBRIDGESHIRE.

(SPEED, "THE THEATRE OF THE EMPIRE OF GREAT BRITAIN," 1611.)

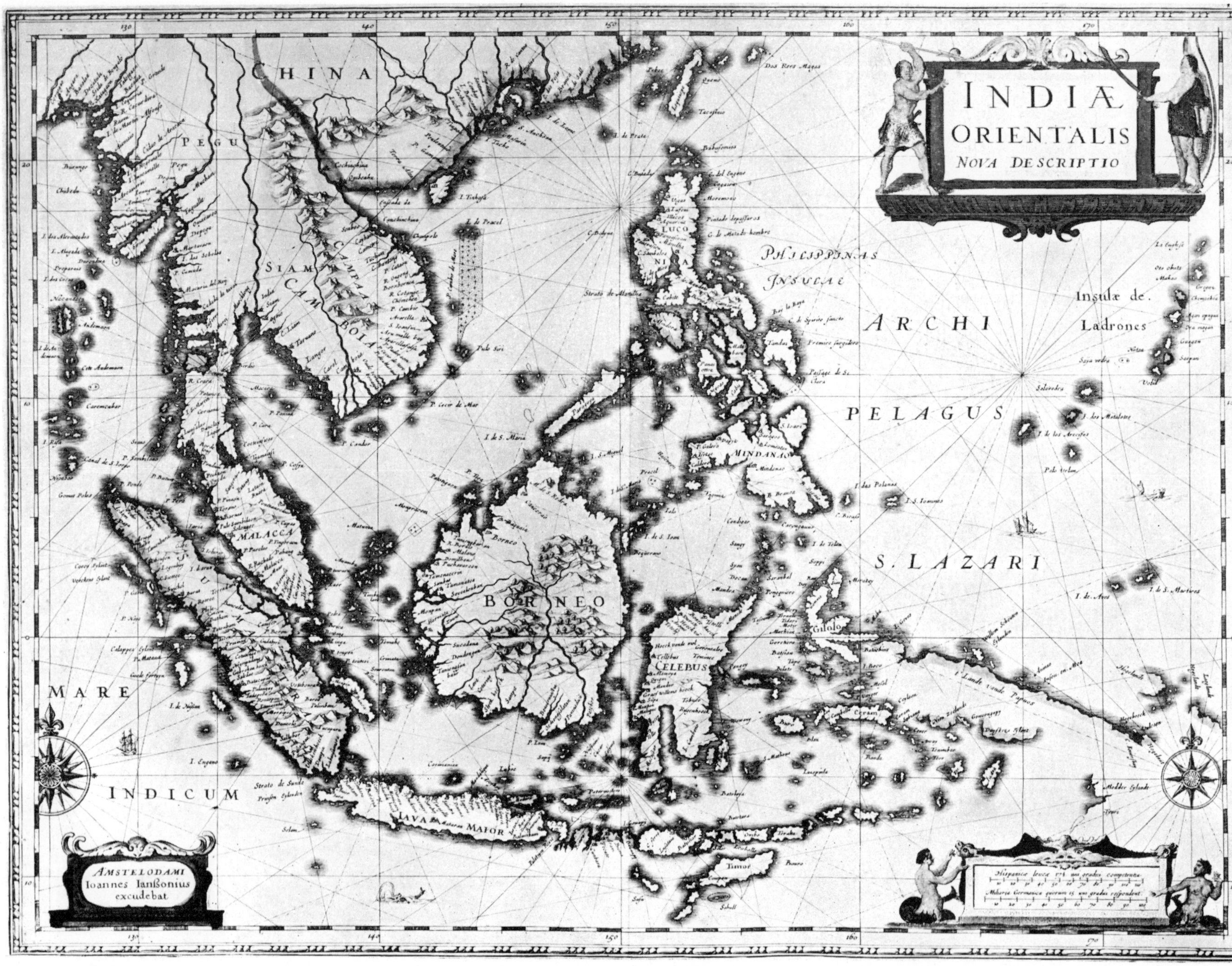

THE INDIAN ARCHIPELAGO.
(MERCATOR'S ATLAS, *Amsterdam*, 1633.)

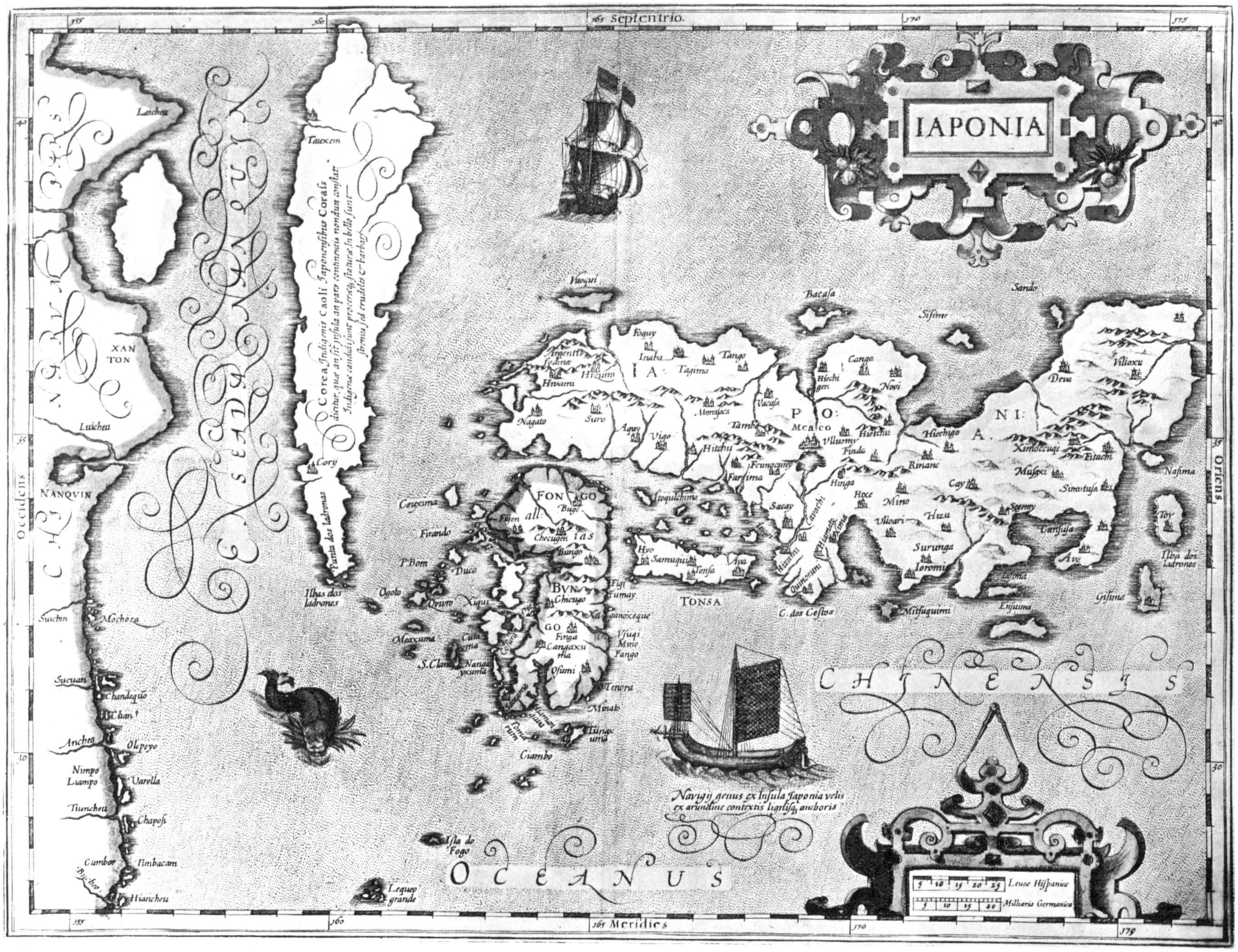

JAPAN.
(MERCATOR'S ATLAS, *Amsterdam*, 1633.)

VIRGINIA AND FLORIDA.
(Mercator's Atlas, *Amsterdam*, 1633.)

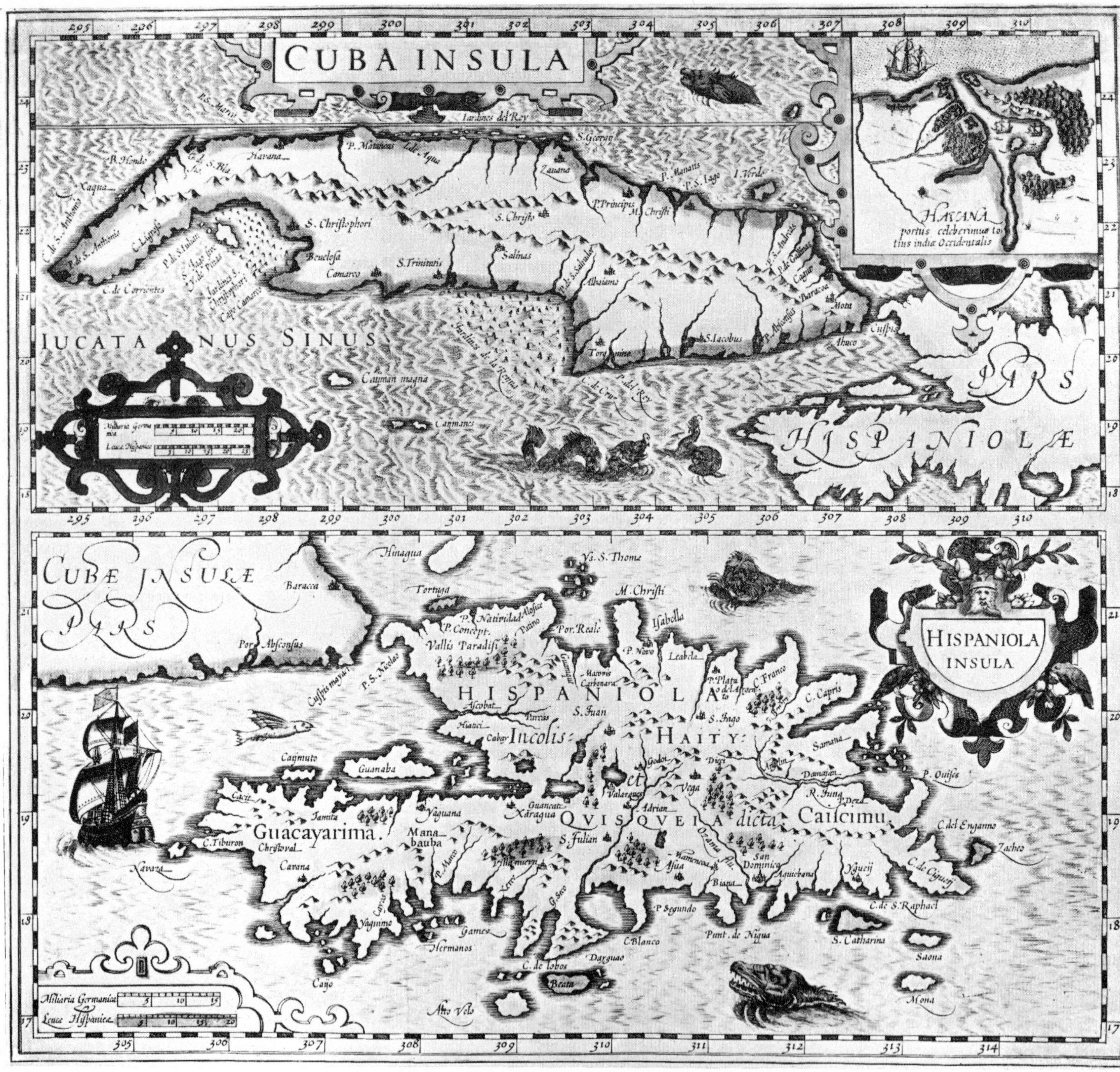

THE ISLANDS OF CUBA AND HISPANIOLA (HAYTI.)
(MERCATOR'S ATLAS, *Amsterdam,* 1633.)

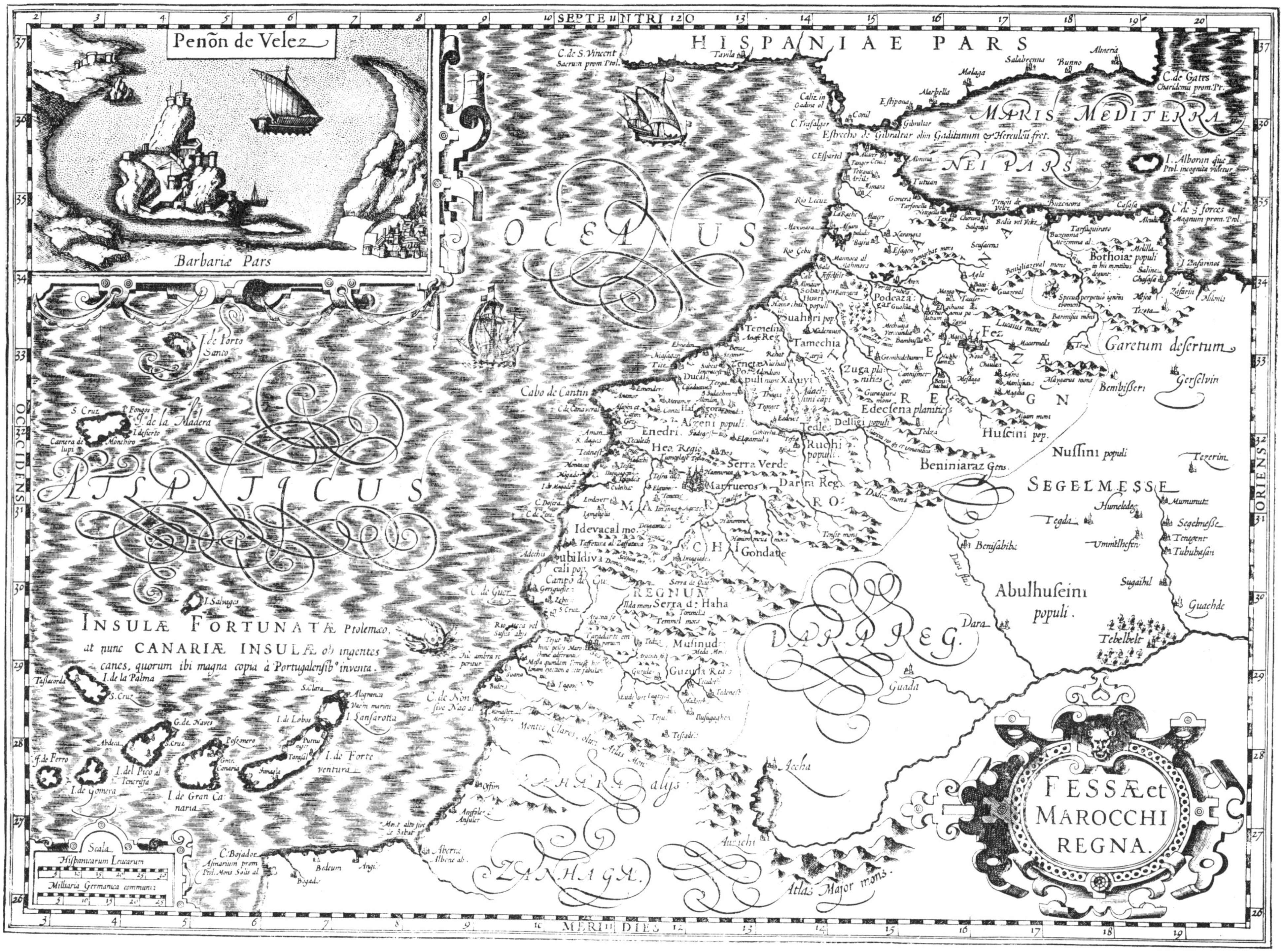

THE KINGDOMS OF FEZ AND MOROCCO.
(MERCATOR'S ENGLISH ATLAS, 1636.)

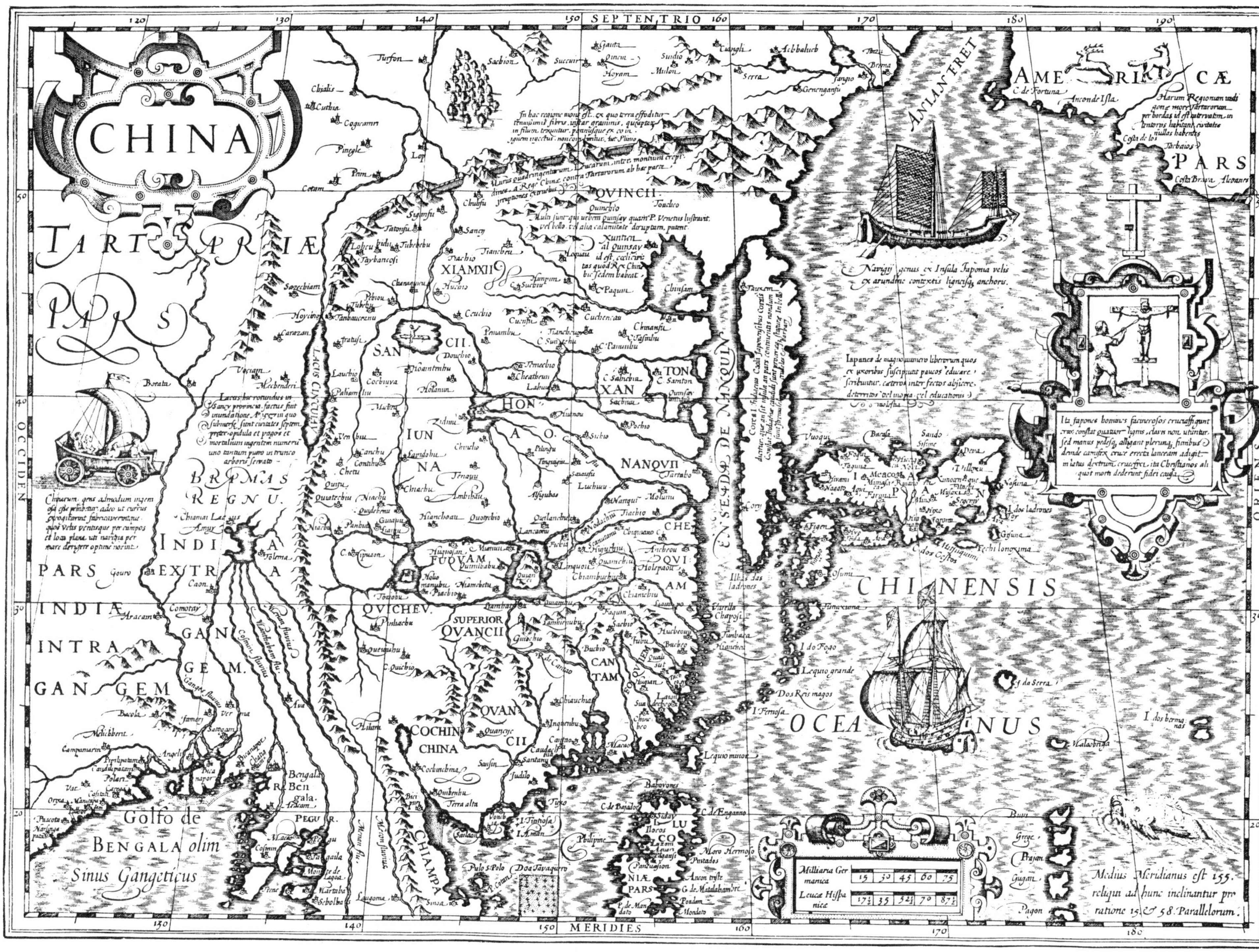

CHINA.
(MERCATOR'S ENGLISH ATLAS, 1636.)

NEW ENGLAND.
(MERCATOR, "HISTORIA MUNDI," 1635.)

VIRGINIA.
(MERCATOR, "HISTORIA MUNDI," 1635.)

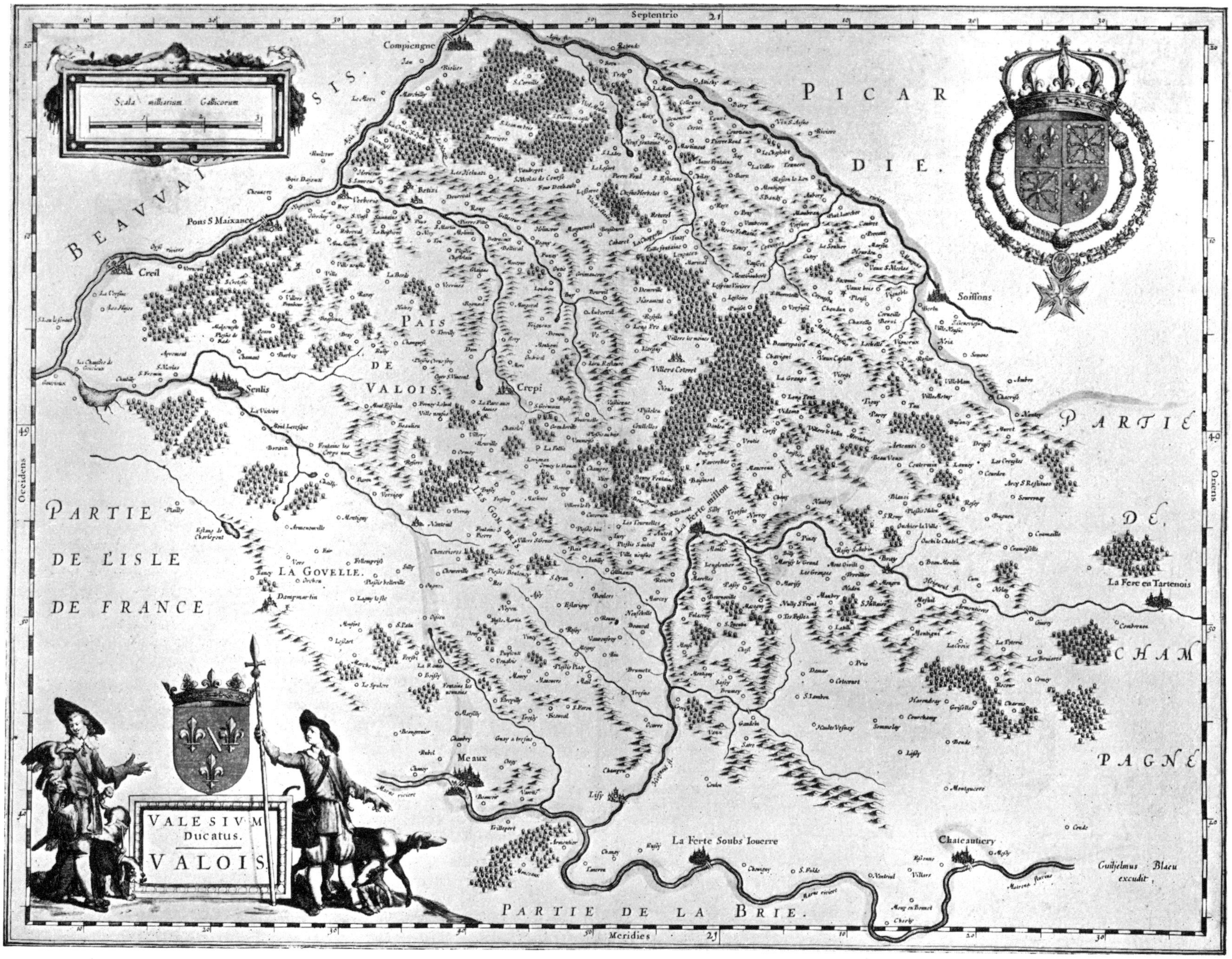

VALOIS.
(W. J. & J. Blaeu, "Nieuwe Atlas," 1642-3.)

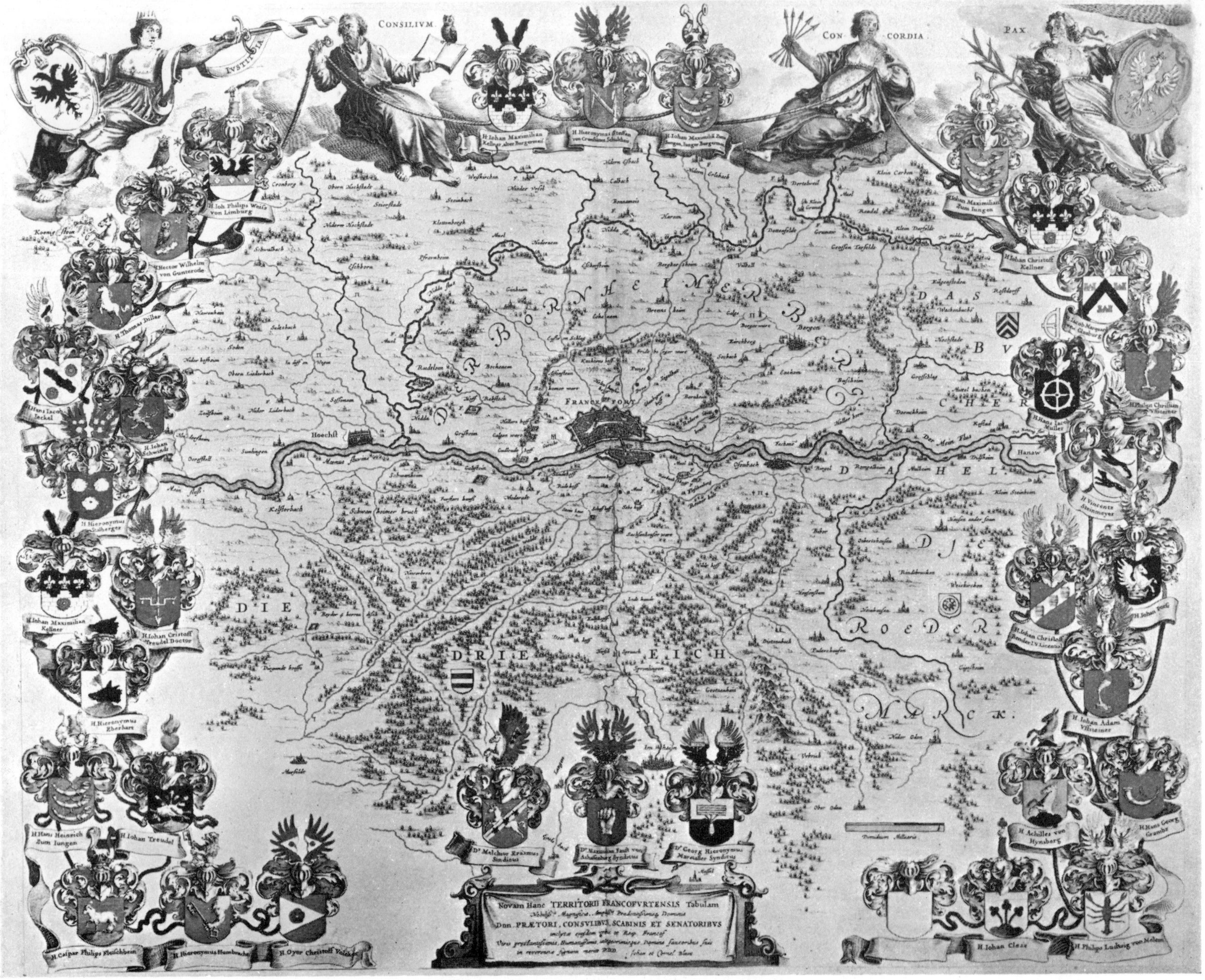

THE TERRITORY OF FRANKFORT ON THE MAIN.
(W. J. & J. BLAEU, "NIEUWE ATLAS," 1642-3.)

NORTH AND SOUTH AMERICA.
(W. J. & J. BLAEU, "NIEUWE ATLAS," 1642-3.)

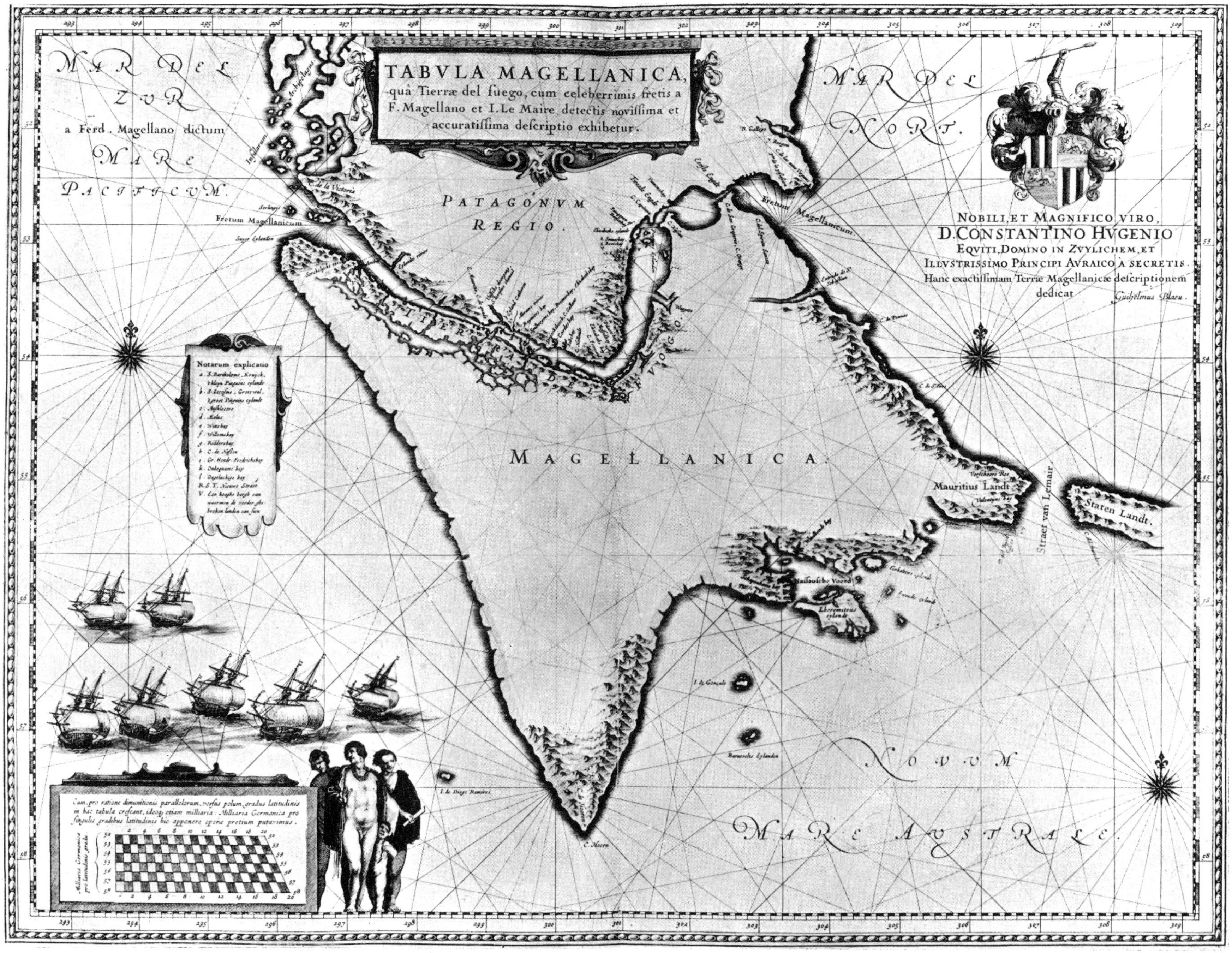

THE STRAITS OF MAGELLAN AND TIERRA DEL FUEGO.
(W. J. & J. BLAEU, "NIEUWE ATLAS," 1642-3.)

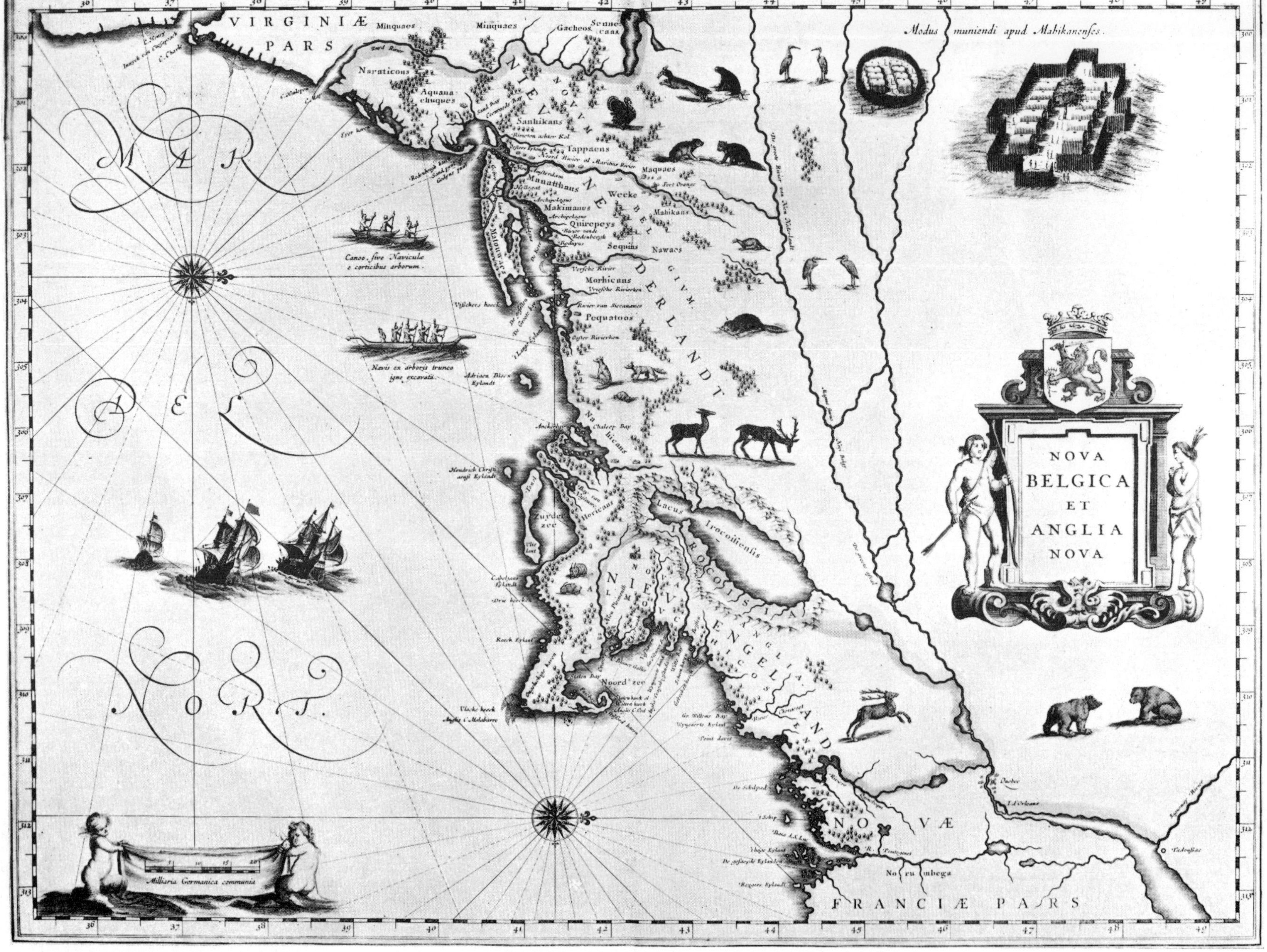

NEW BELGIUM AND NEW ENGLAND.

(W. J. & J. BLAEU, "NIEUWE ATLAS," 1642-3.)

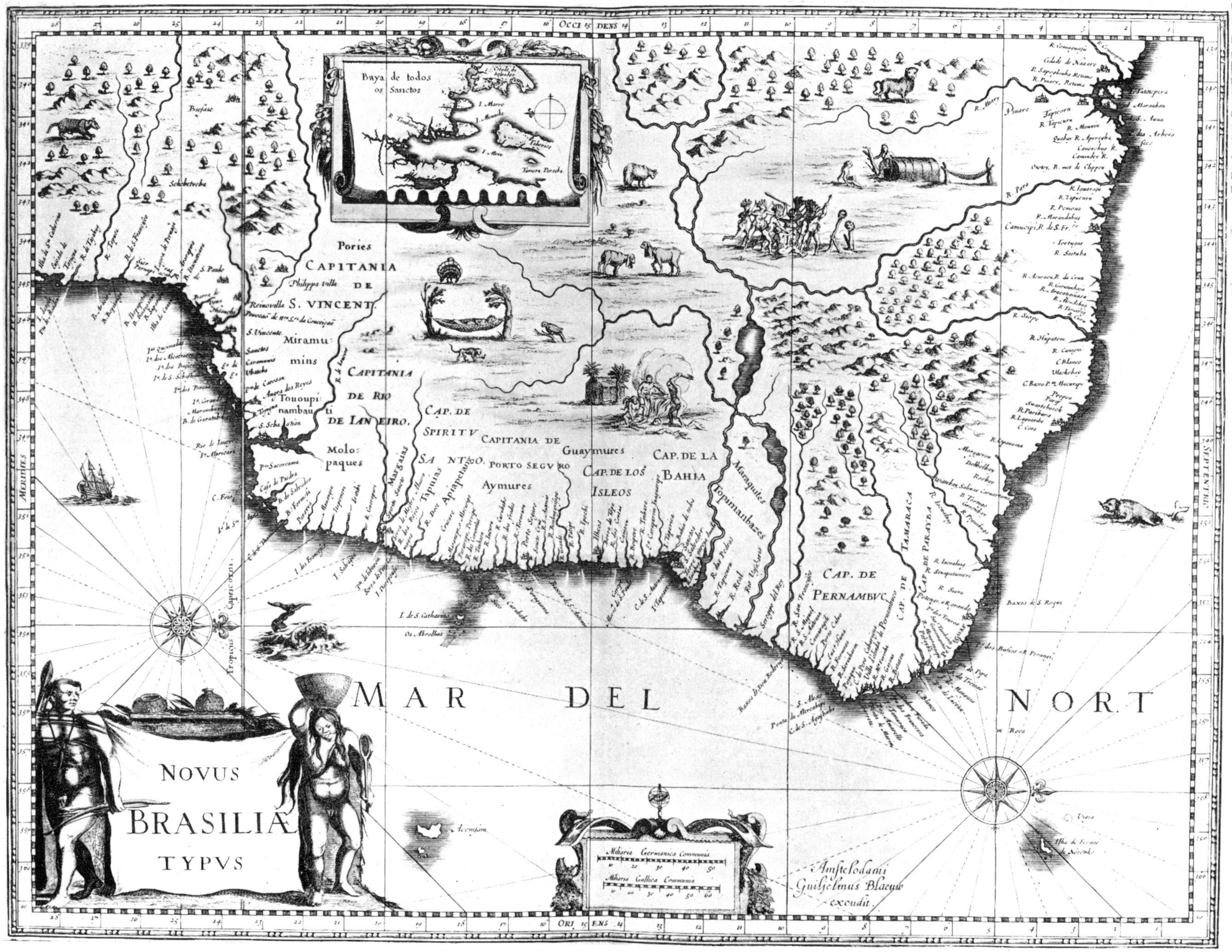

BRAZIL.

(W. J. & J. Blaeu, "Nieuwe Atlas," 1642-3.)

Picardy, 1635

OXFORDSHIRE, 1646

Jan Jansson's elegant map follows the tradition of John Speed's map by incorporating the coats of arms of the colleges and using gowned academics in the titlepiece design.

CALIFORNIA, 1666

Approximately 2/3rds of Pieter Goos' beautifully engraved map of the island, California. The original plate extends westwards into the Pacific. This is one of the first maps to concentrate on the area and appeared in one of the most sumptuous seen atlas productions. Goos' atlas was reprinted several times before 1697 but few examples of the maps appear on the market nowadays.

THE MID NORTH EAST AMERICAN COAST, 1666

Goos' elegant chart of the coast from Chesapeake to Cape Cod is one of the first to provide detail of Long Island and the Hudson mouth.

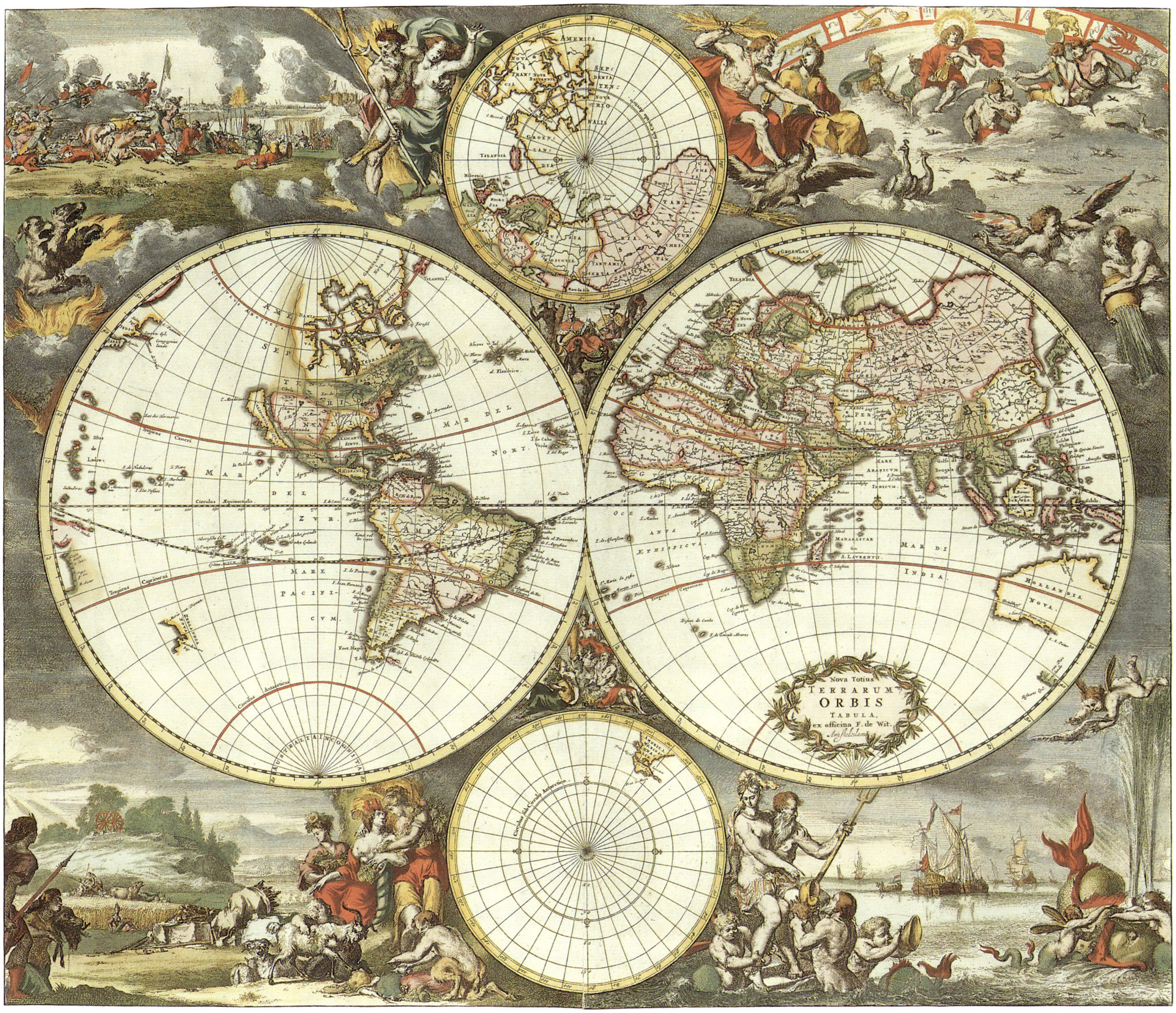

The World, c 1670

Frederic de Wit's fine double hemisphere map apeared in his atlases of sea charts over about the next thirty years. The decoration surrounding the spheres was etched by one of the foremost engravers of the time, Romeyn de Hooghe, and shows by allegorical representation images of fire, earth, water and air.

North and South America, c 1685

Johannes de Ram's finely engraved map, published in Amsterdam, shows California as an Island but is also notable for its decorative title cartouche showing native American Indians, gold ingots, serpents and birds.

THE CHESAPEAKE, DELAWARE AND JERSEY COASTLINES, 1689

William Mount and Thomas Page issued this detailed chart in *The English Pilot-Fourth Book*. This publication was first issued in 1689 and, with additional charts, throughout the next century. Each of its five volumes covered the coasts of different areas of the world and presented the English seafarer with more detailed charts than previously available of many areas. (Approx 31½ × 20ins.)

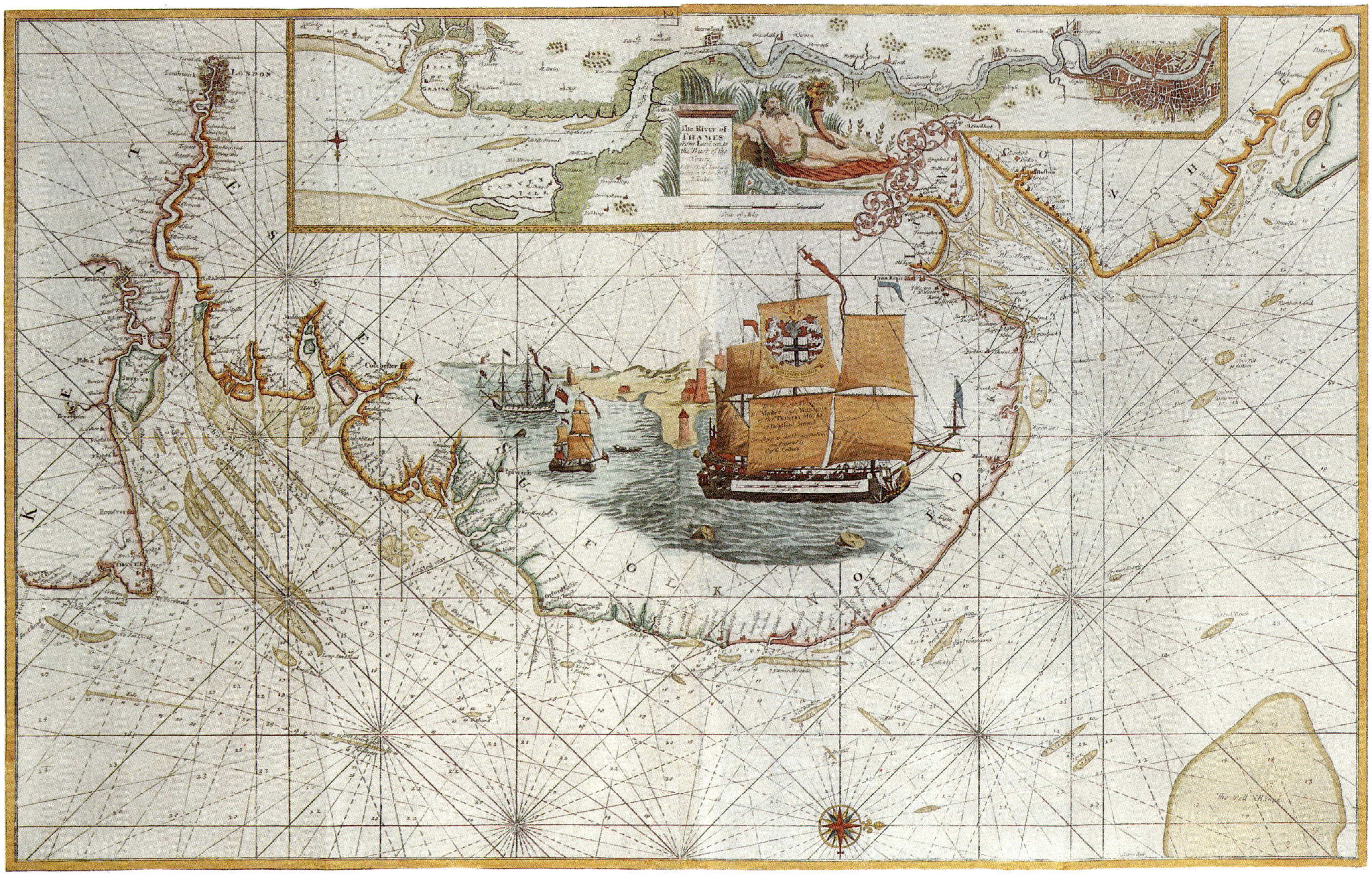

THE EAST COAST AND THAMES ESTUARY, 1693

Captain Greenville Collins' atlas of sea charts of the British coasts was the first systematic survey of our coastline. This particularly elaborate chart is dedicated to the Master and Wardens of Trinity House for whom the work was carried out. (Approx 37 × 23½ins.)

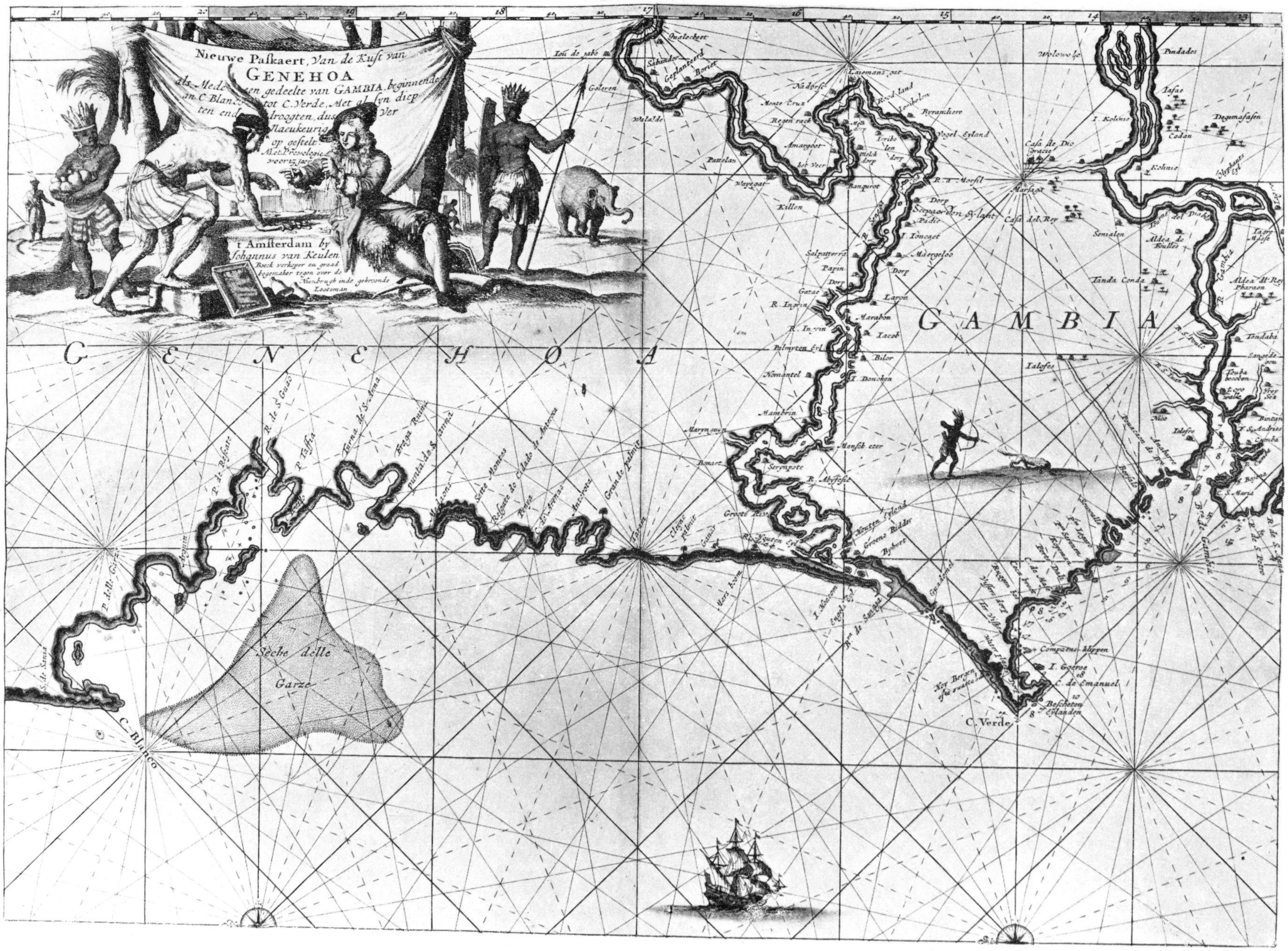

CHART OF THE COAST OF GUINEA.
(Van Keulen, "Sea Atlas," 1682.)

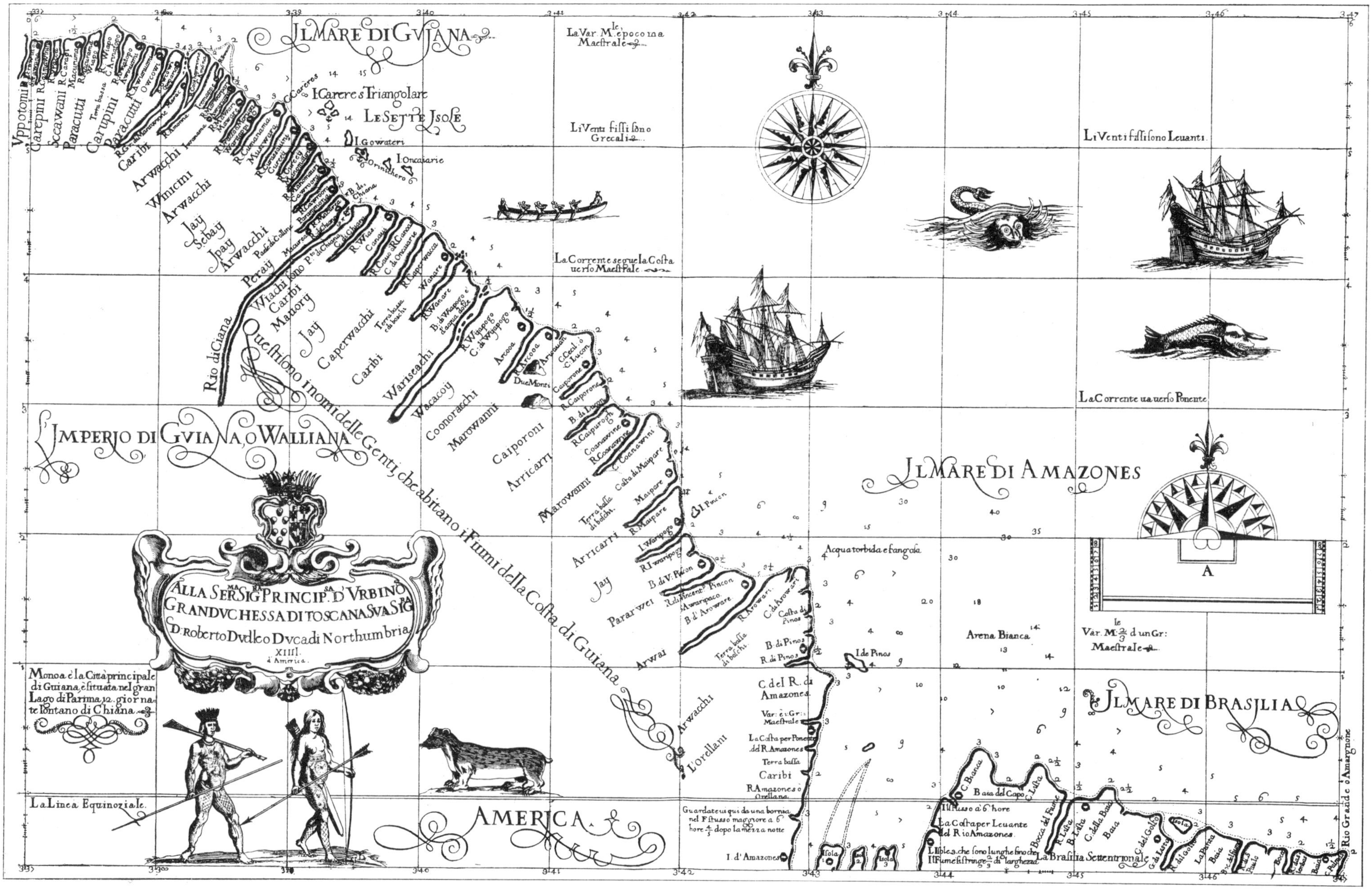

CHART OF THE COAST OF GUIANA.
(Dudley, "Dell' Arcano del Mare," 1646-7.)

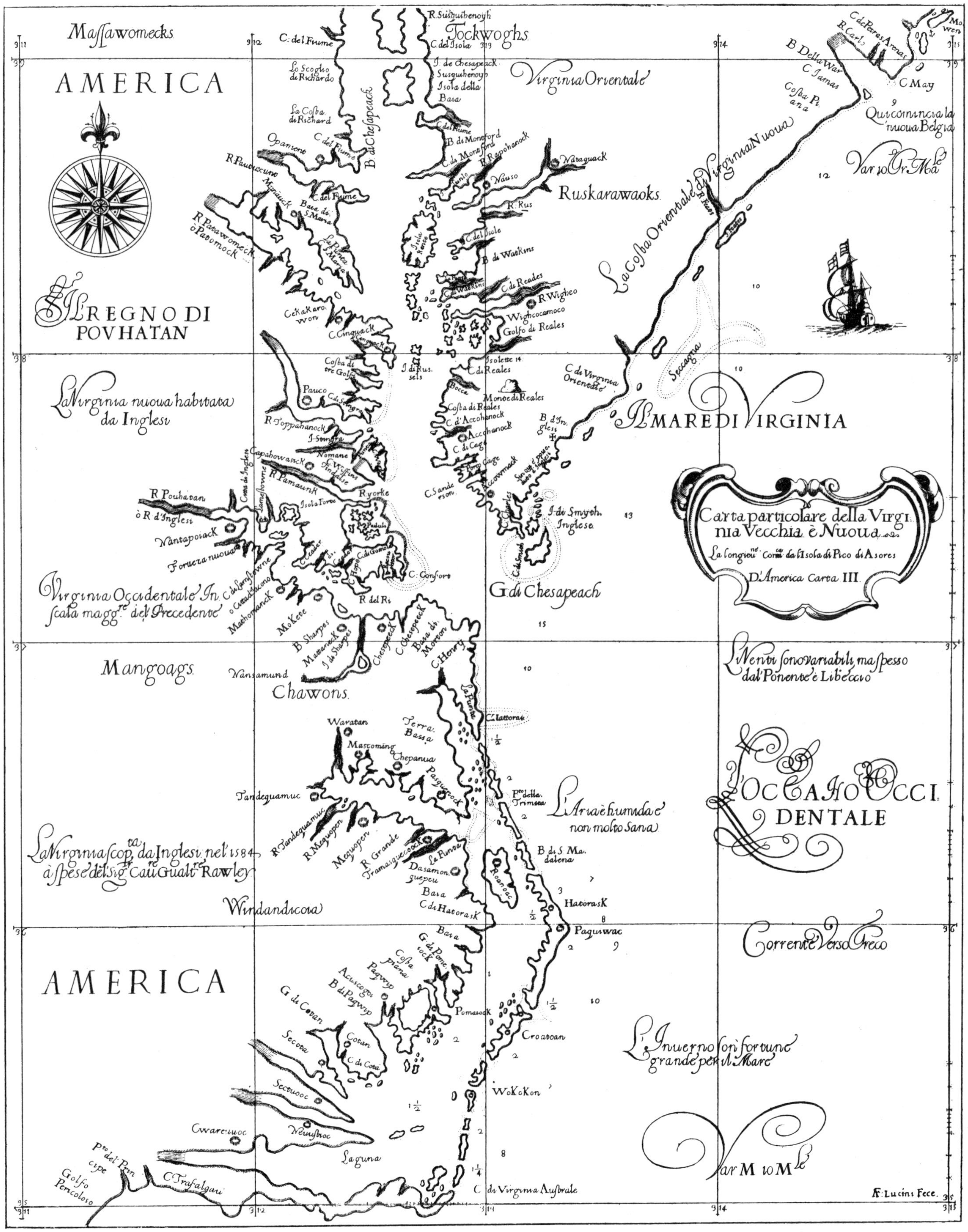

OLD AND NEW VIRGINIA.
(DUDLEY, "DELL' ARCANO DEL MARE," 1646-7.)

THE COUNTY OF ESSEX.
(JANSSON, "NOVUS ATLAS," 1658.)

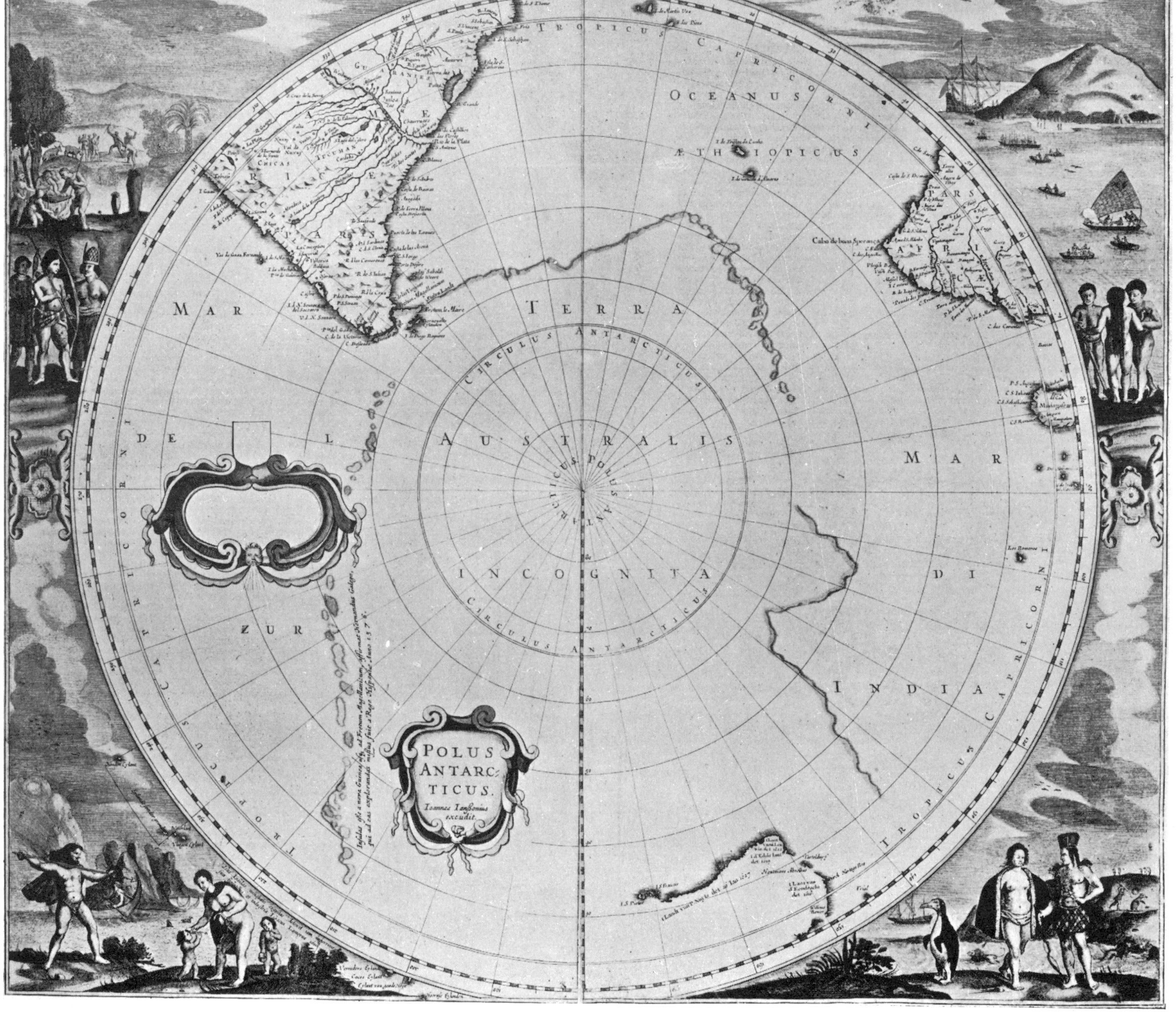

THE SOUTH POLAR REGIONS.
(JANSSON, "NOVUS ATLAS," 1658.)

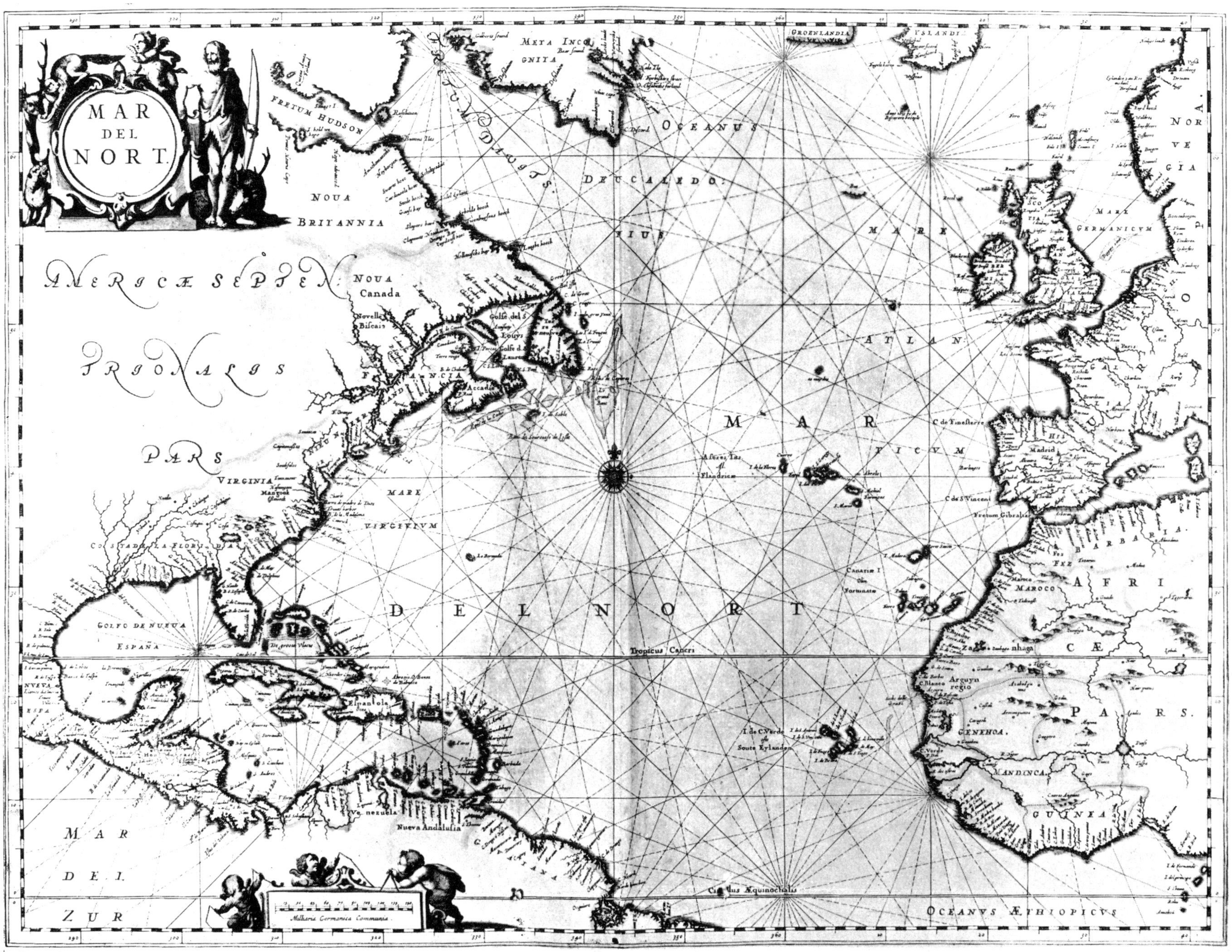

CHART OF THE NORTH ATLANTIC.
(JANSSON, "NOVUS ATLAS," 1658.)

TITLE PAGE TO
PIETER GOOS, "ZEE-ATLAS," 1666.

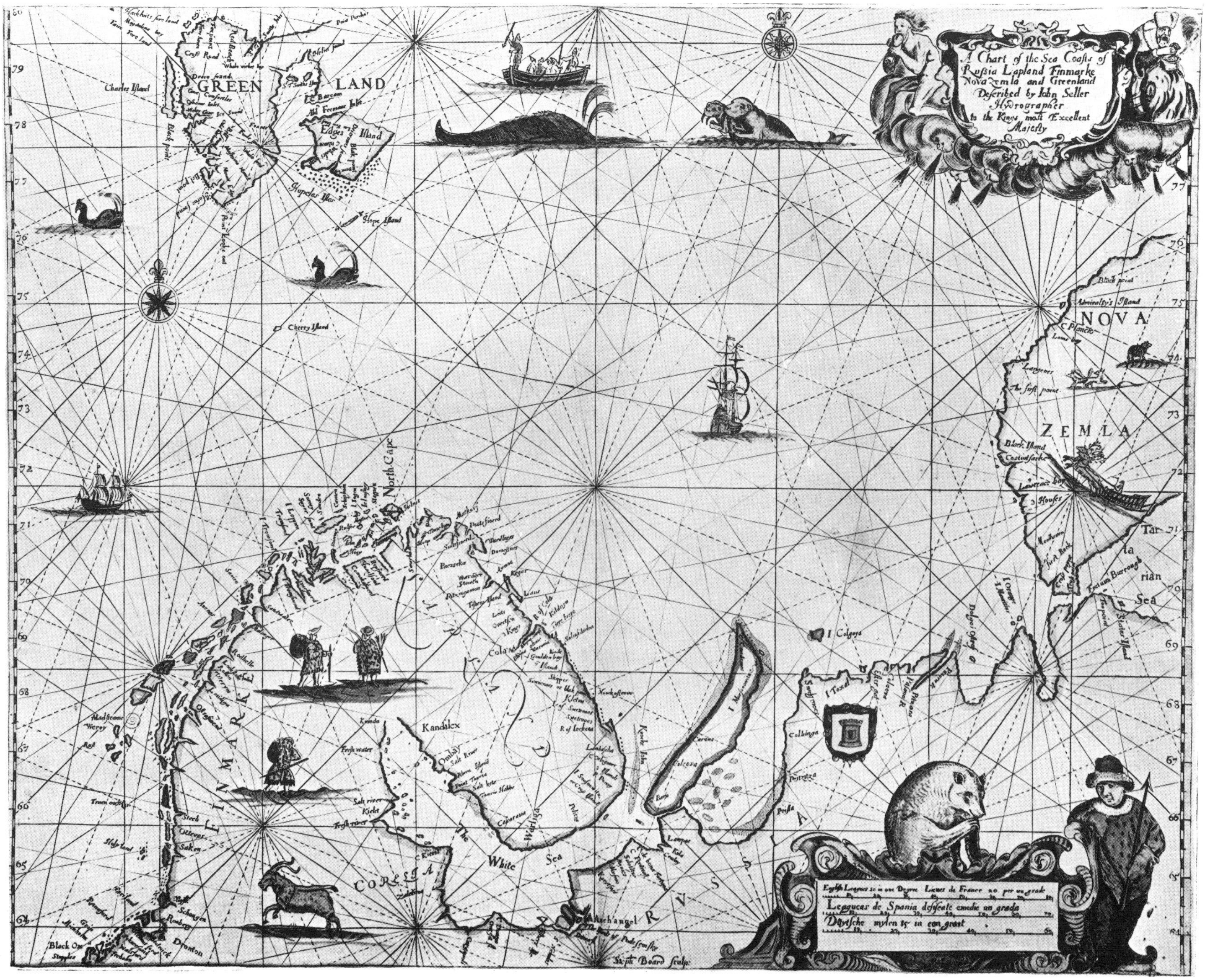

CHART OF THE SEA COAST OF RUSSIA, LAPLAND, ETC.
(SELLER, "THE ENGLISH PILOT," 1671-5.)

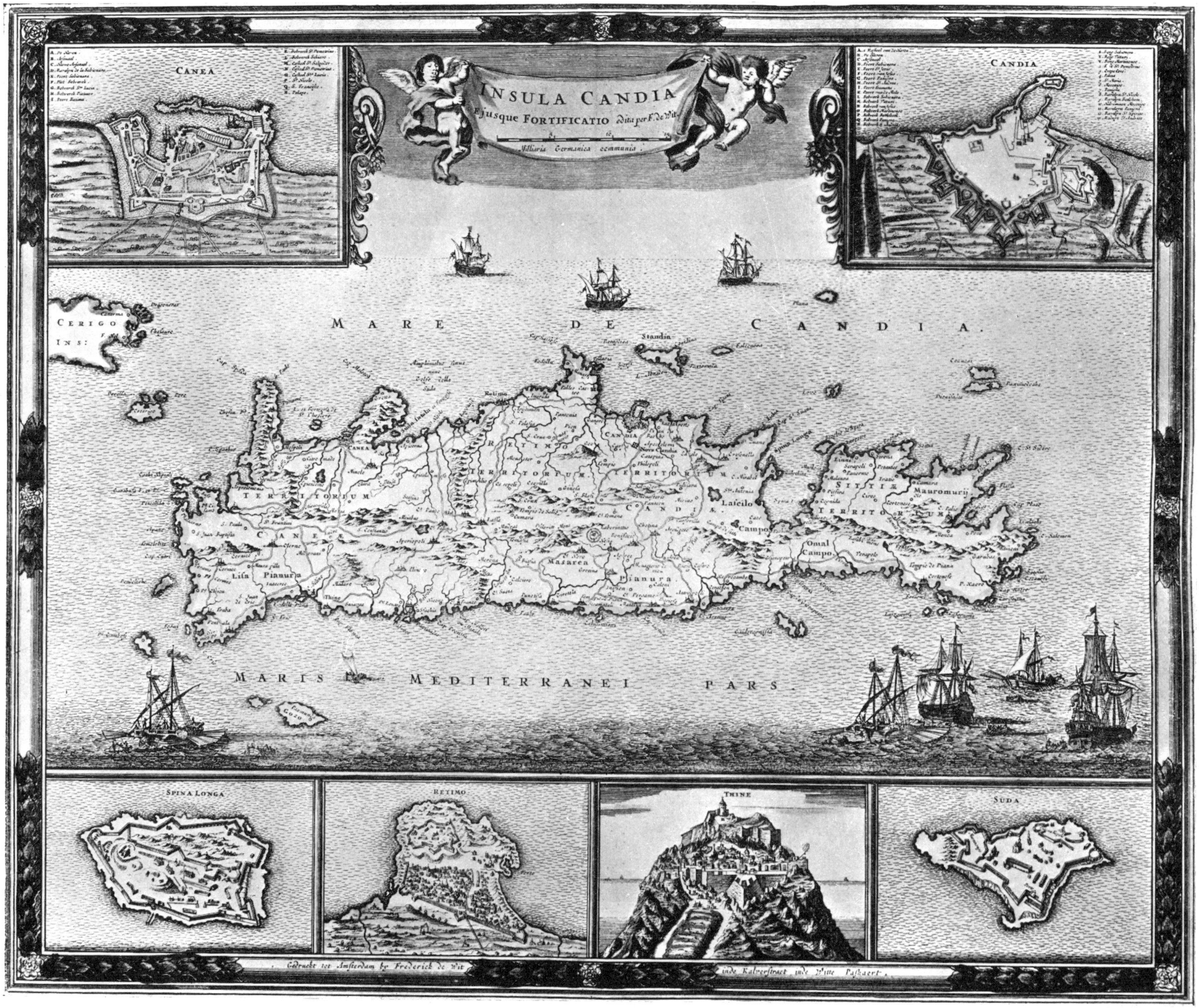

THE ISLAND OF CANDIA (CRETE).
(F. DE WIT, ATLAS, *c.* 1688.)

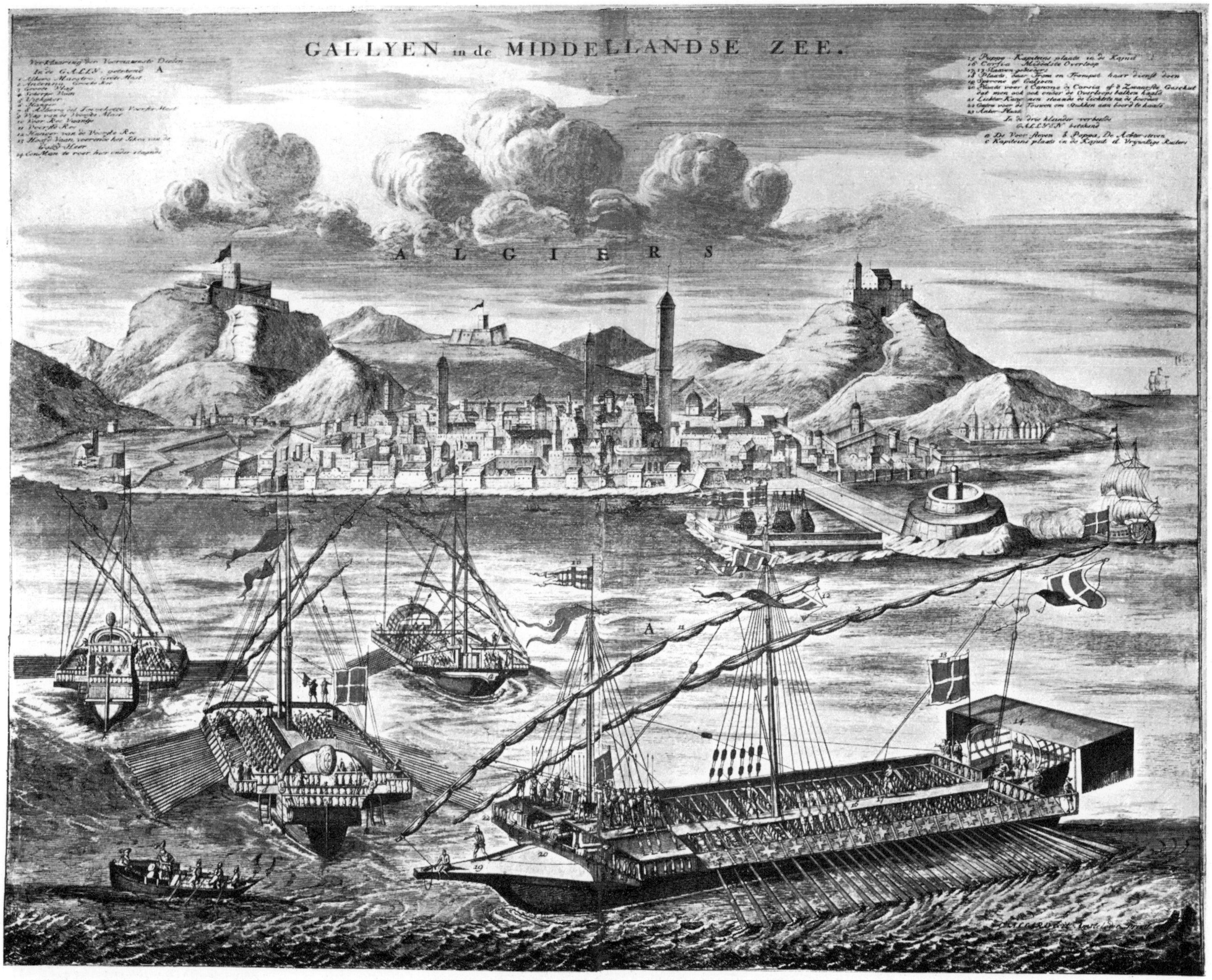

ALGIERS, WITH MEDITERRANEAN GALLEYS.
(VAN KEULEN, DUTCH ATLAS, 1709.)

The numbered explanations refer to details of the largest galley (A):—1, 2, mainmast and yard; 7, 8, 11, foremast and yard; 3, 4, 6, 9, 10, 12, 13, flags, pendants and ensigns; 14, 15, covered poop; 16, 17, central gangway with slave controllers; 18, drummers and trumpeters; 19-23, beakhead, guns, anchors, etc.

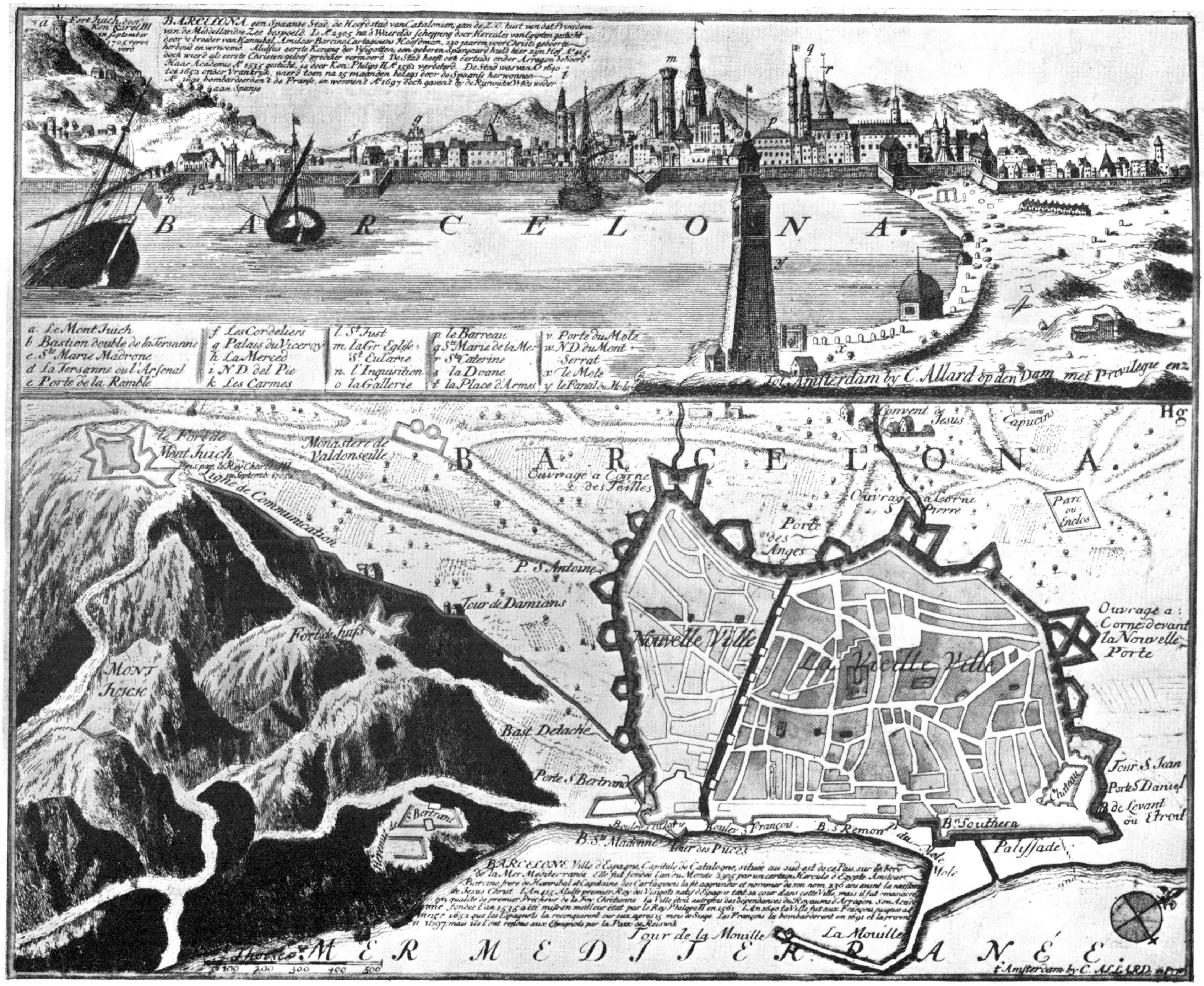

BARCELONA.
(Schenck, "Atlas Contractus," 1713.)

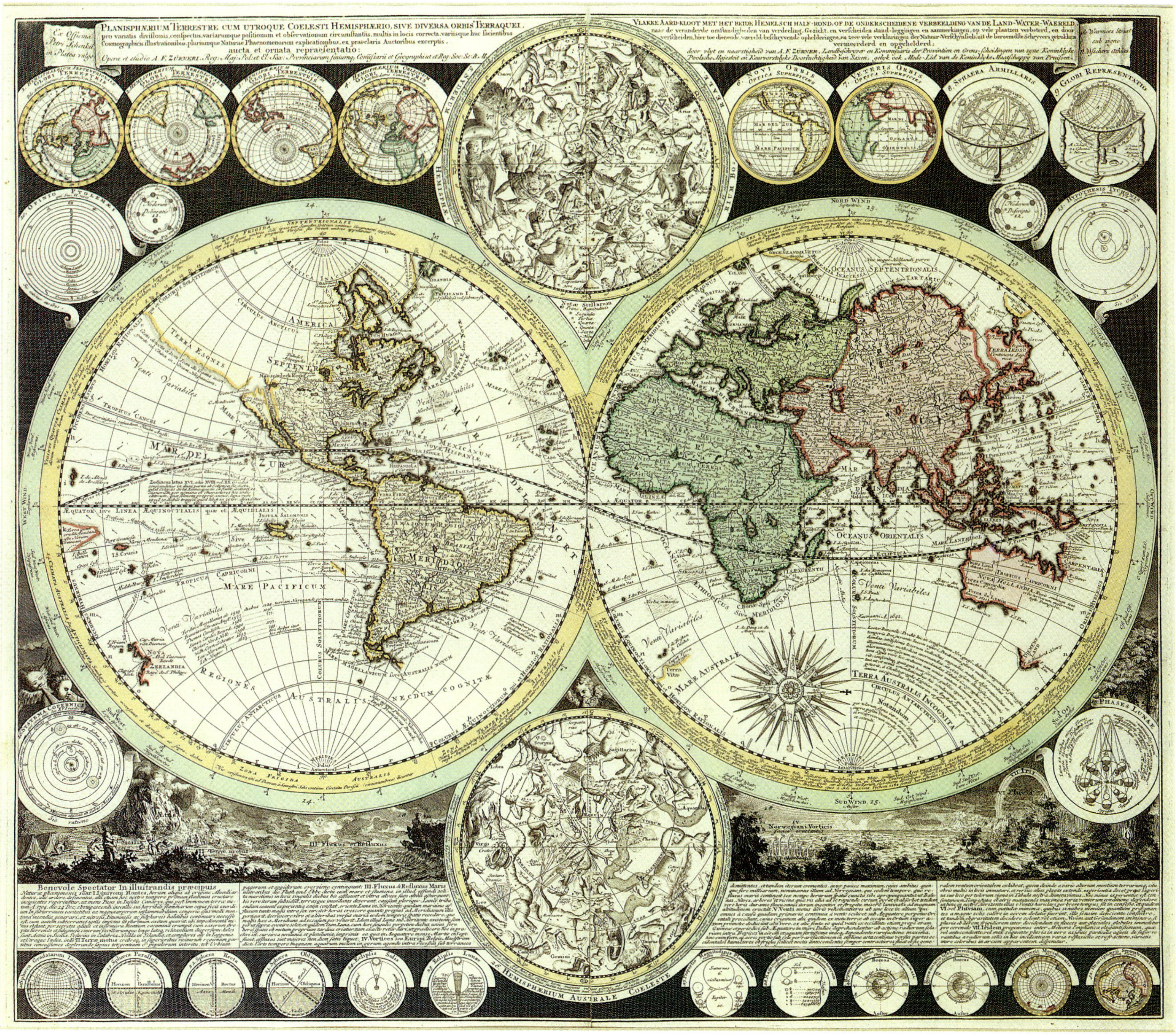

THE WORLD, c 1700

A.F. Zumer's map published in Amsterdam indicates a move away from the lavish decoration so typical of Dutch map production at the end of the seventeenth century. The map is a wealth of cartographic and geographical detail, the illustration below the two major spheres being of meteorological and physical phenomena.

THE INDIAN OCEAN, AUSTRALIA AND THE ORIENT, c 1700

A magnificent chart from the van Kevlen publishing house encompassing an area of particular interest to European entrepreneurs of the time. The Australian coastline is shown in a form not to be improved till the end of the eighteenth century when Cook, Flanders, Bass and others completed the eastern and southern detail.

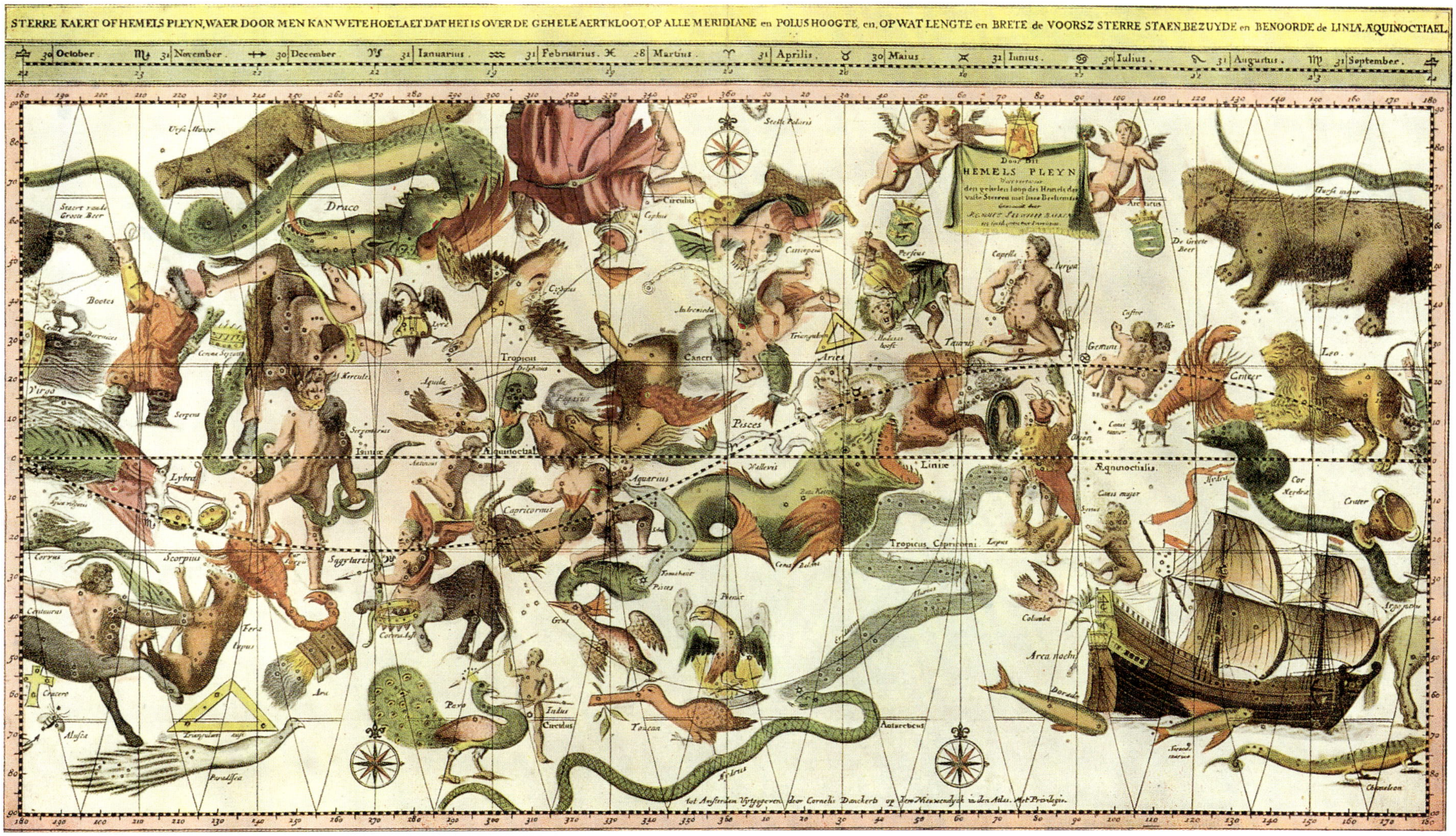

Celestial Planisphere, 1704

This fine chart by R.T. Backer was published by J. Danckerts and other Amsterdam publishers until as late as 1792. The typical figured forms for the constellations were adopted from earliest times and are still popular today.

Southern Hemisphere Star Chart, c 1710

Carel Allard's chart is one of a pair and includes, around the central chart, diagrams of an eclipse, the sun, the moon and various planetary systems.

North Western Italy, c 1710

A magnificent large scale map of the Piedmont area published by Pierre Mortier on Amsterdam. This and other notble maps of areas of European military activity appeared in Mortic's issues of A.H. Jaillot's atlas of world maps and, as in this instance, often incorporate spectacular title pieces. This fascinating scene shows an army, under the supervision of Prince Eugene of Savoy (to whom the map is dedicated), passing through the Alps. Pulleys can be seen in operation lifting heavy pieces of equipment and each part is occupied by marching soldiers. (Approx. 24 × 38ins.)

North America, c 1720

Herman Molt's large scale map is one of the most sought-after of the period. The scale of the map allows for good detail to be shown, some bizarre, some up-to-date. The insets at the left side detail major ports and harbours and the annotated scene describes the cod fishing industry essential to the north east coastal economy. (Approx 38 × 23½ins.)

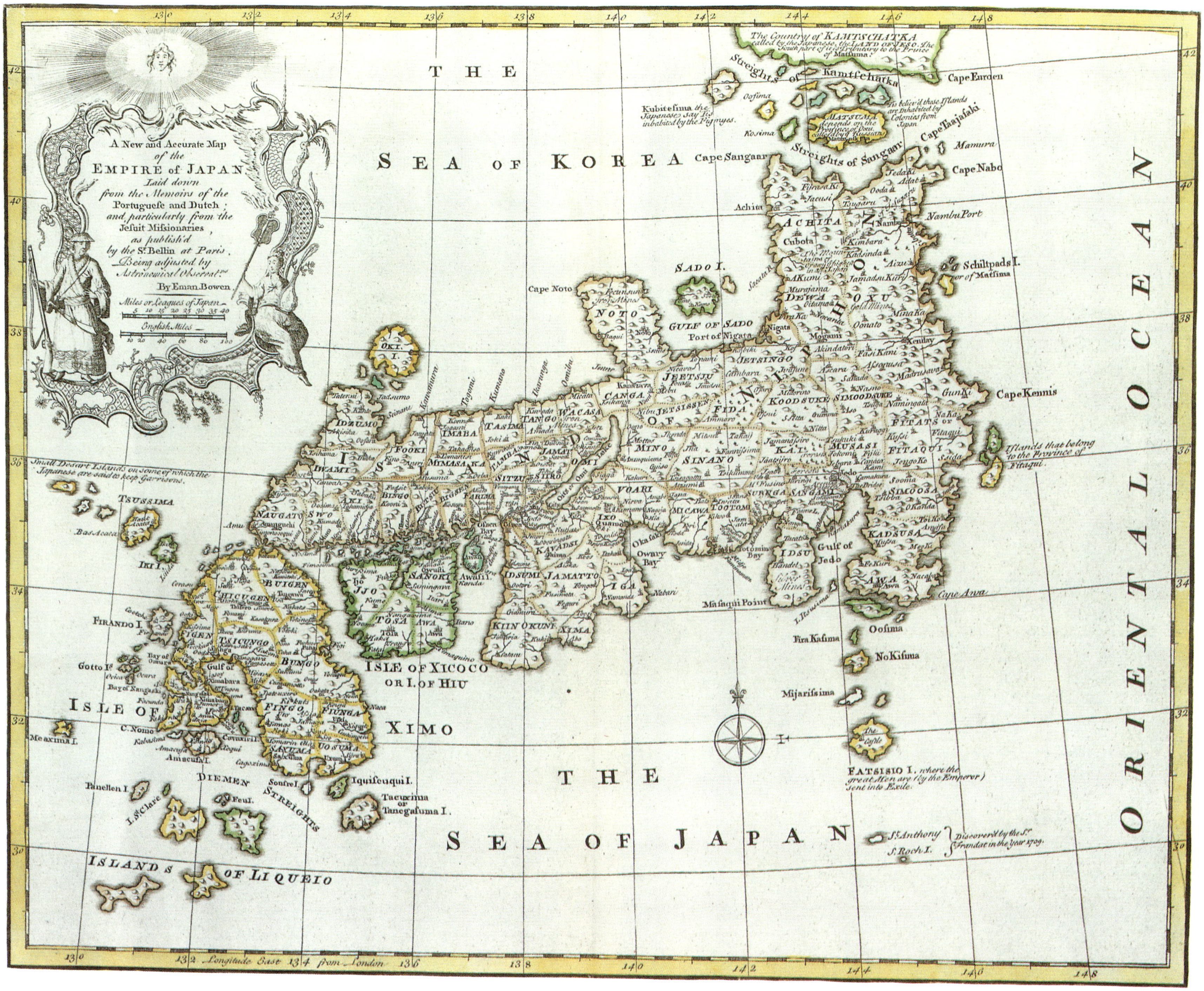

JAPAN, 1747

Emanuel Bowen's detailed map is based primarily on reports from the Jesuit Missionaries, the only Europeans allowed access to the interior of the country at this time. The map appeared in Bowen's *A Complete Systems of Geography*, a comprehensive two-volume work describing, with some 69 maps, the whole world.

Arabia, c 1815

John Thomson *New General Atlas* was one of several large format, detailed works produced at the start of the nineteenth century. Although the maps lack decoration they are attractive and the use of shading indicates here the presence of deserts and mountainous areas.

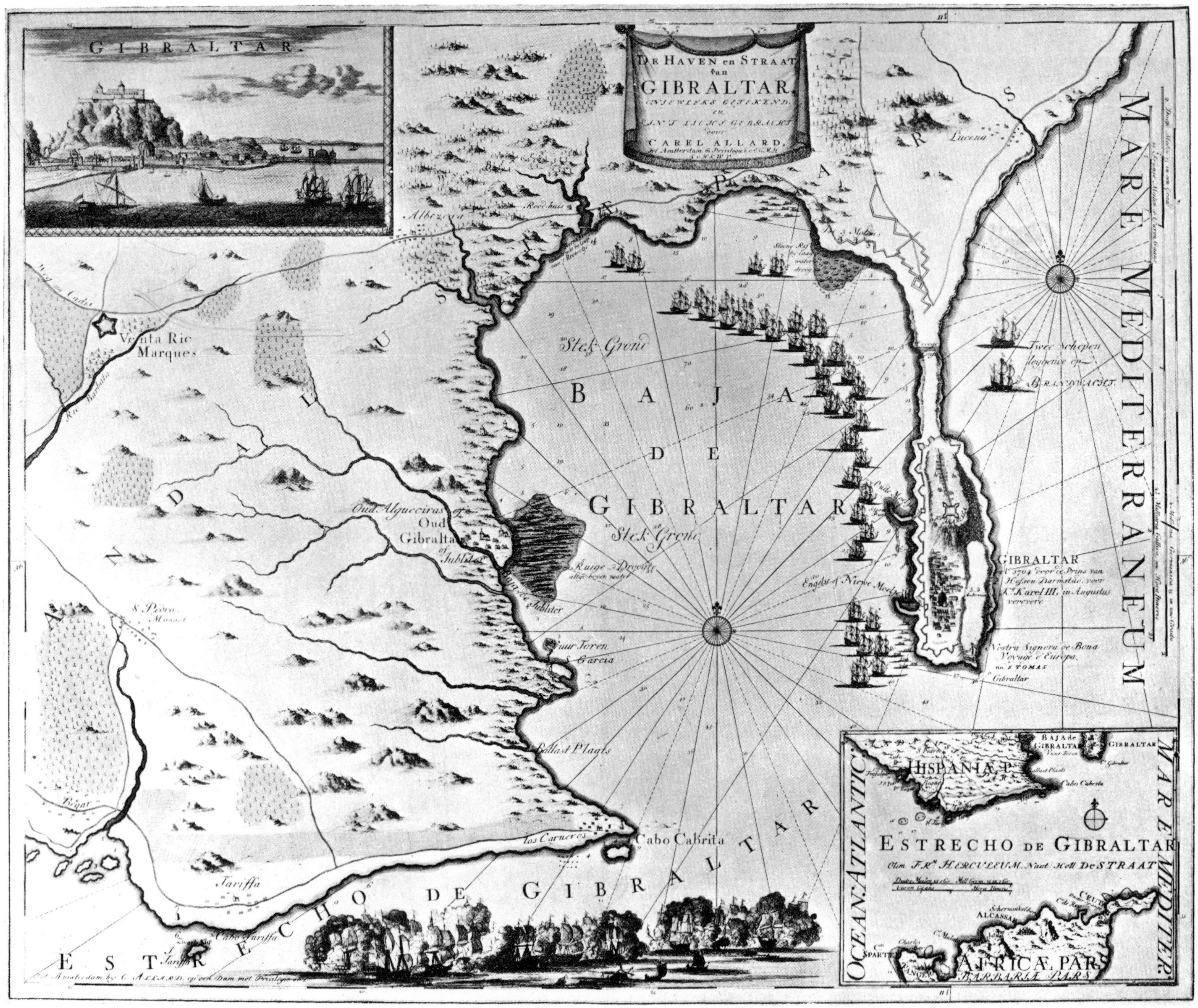

THE HARBOUR AND STRAITS OF GIBRALTAR.
(SCHENCK, "ATLAS CONTRACTUS," 1713.)

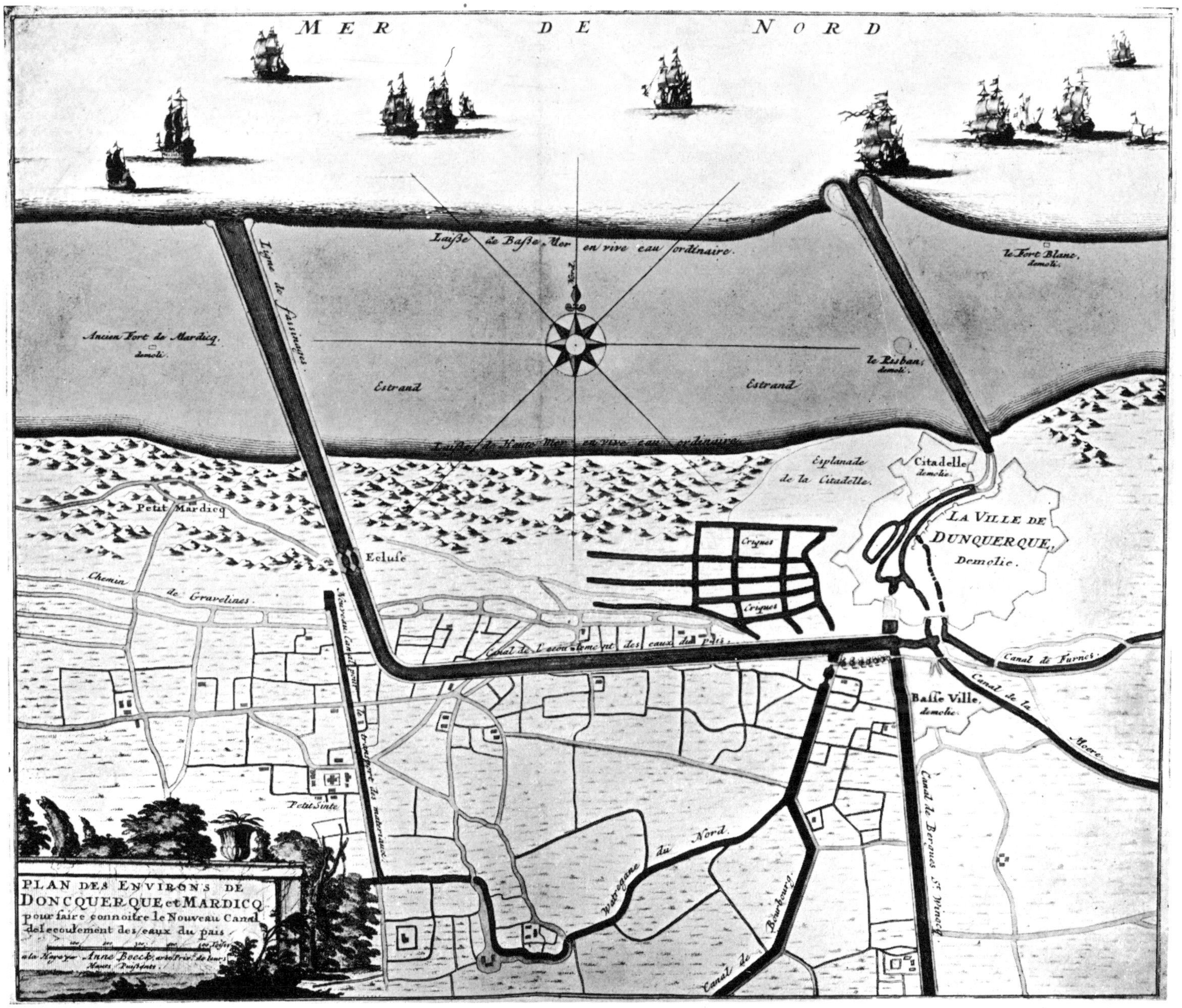

PLAN OF DUNKIRK AND MARDYCK.
(SCHENCK, "ATLAS CONTRACTUS," 1713.)

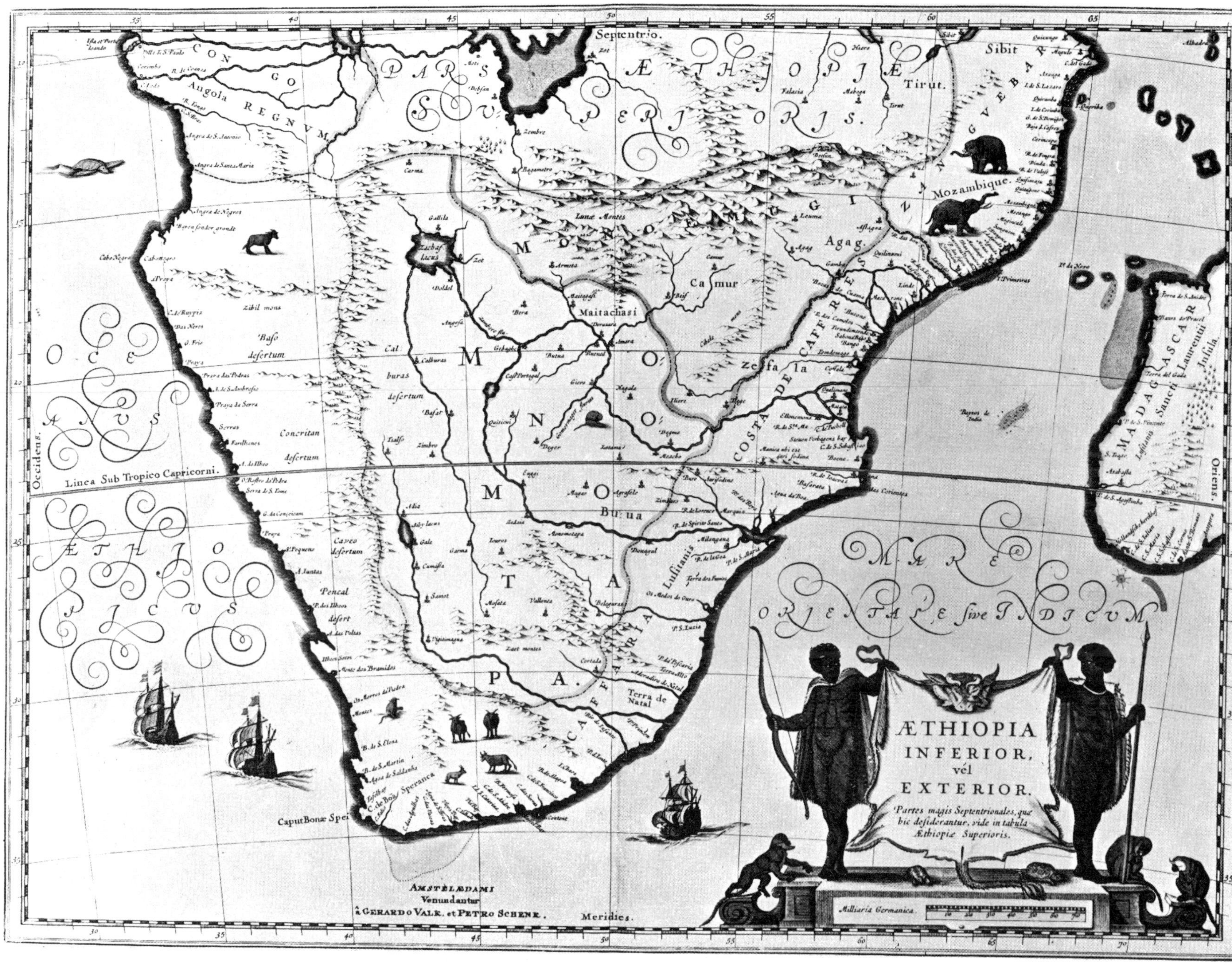

ÆTHIOPIA INFERIOR.
(SCHENCK, "ATLAS CONTRACTUS," 1713.)

ZEALAND, DENMARK.
(Schenck, "Atlas Contractus," 1713.)

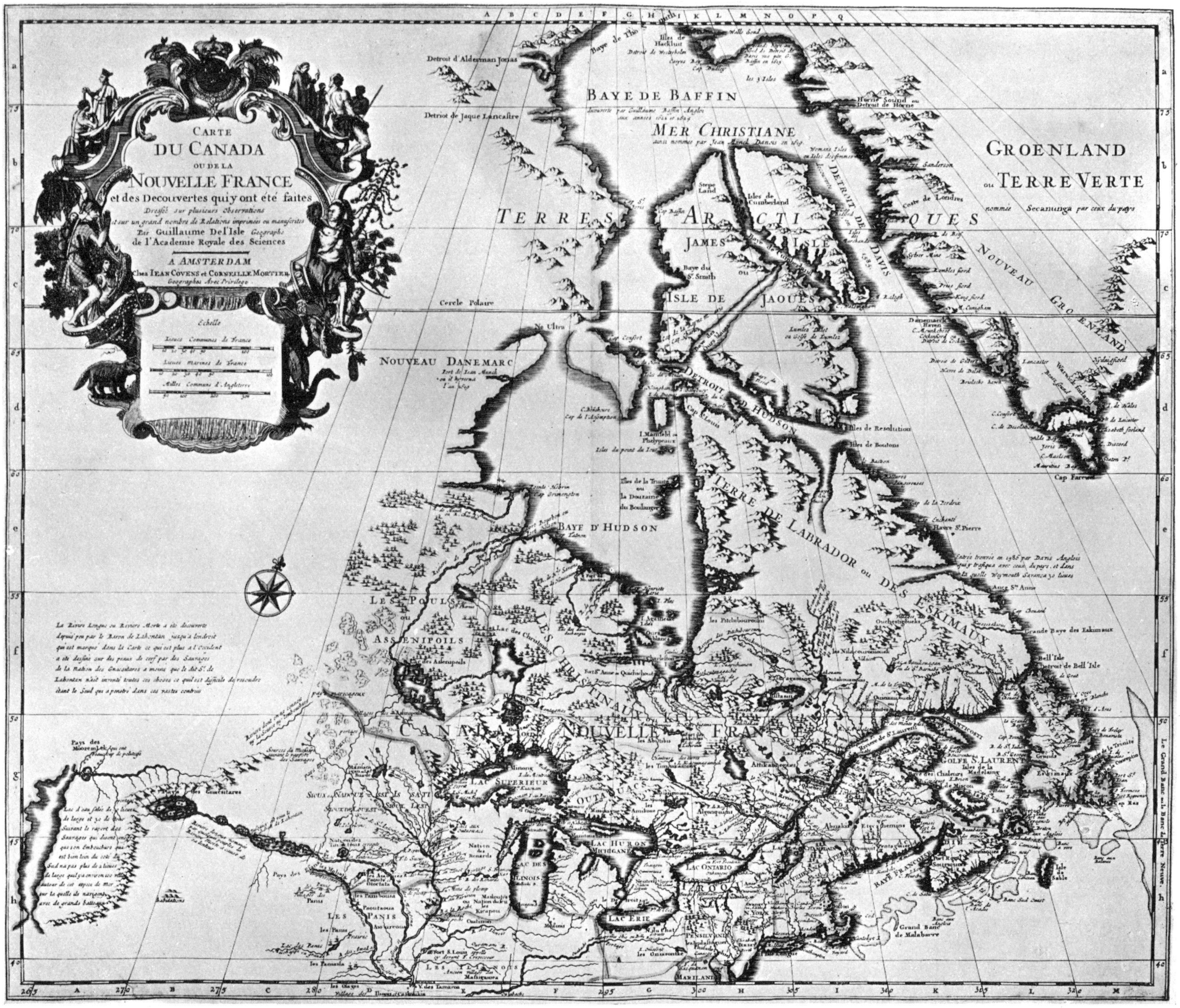

CANADA, OR NEW FRANCE.
(DE LISLE, "ATLAS NOUVEAU," 1737.)

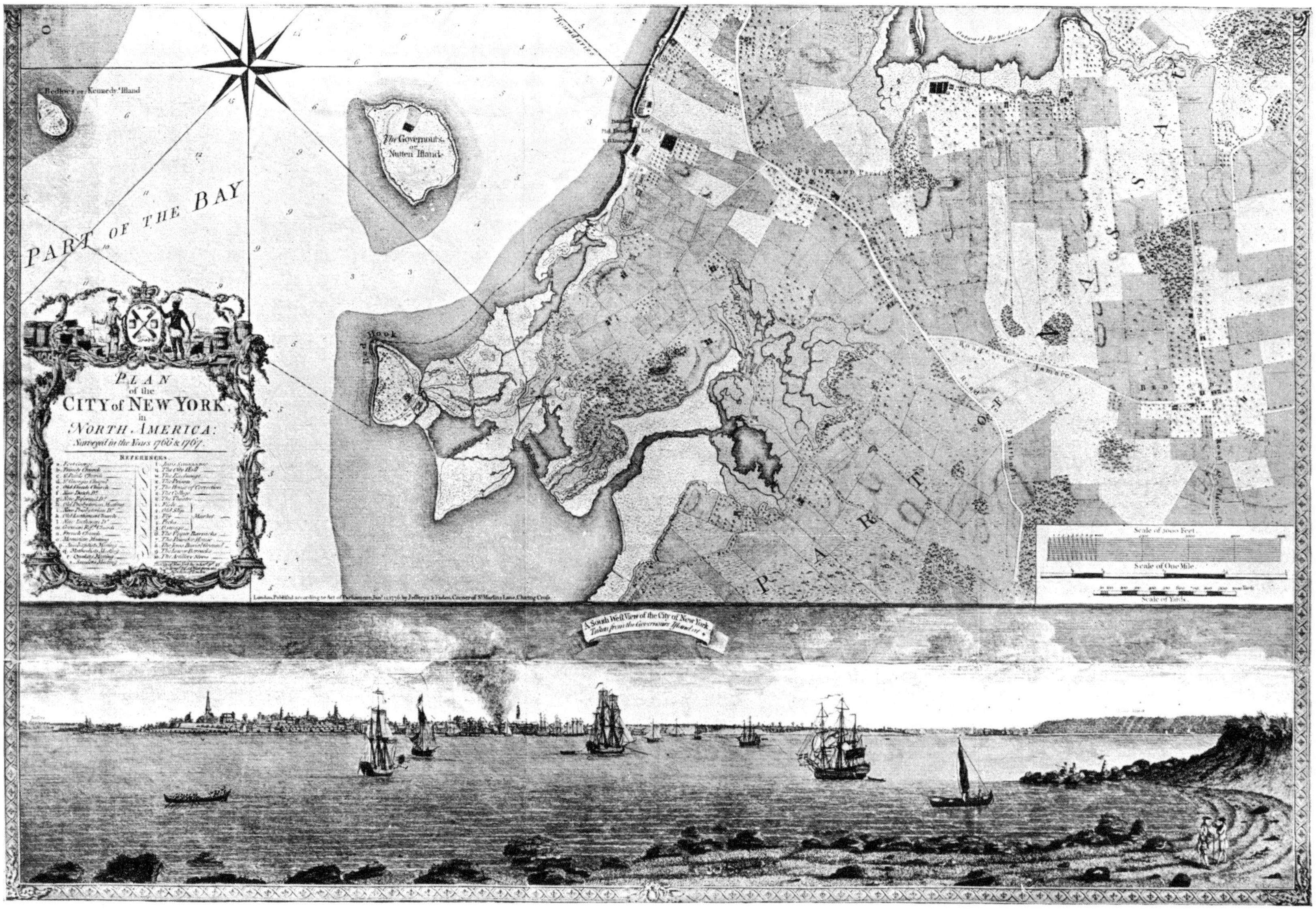

PLAN OF THE CITY OF NEW YORK,
WITH A SOUTH-WEST VIEW OF THE CITY FROM GOVERNOR'S ISLAND.
FROM AN ENGRAVING PUBLISHED IN LONDON BY JEFFERYS & FADEN, JANUARY 12, 1776.

LIST OF BOOKS USEFUL TO COLLECTORS.

ANDREWS (Michael C.). Mediæval maps. (In the Journal of the Manchester Geographical Society, November, 1925).

Mr. Andrews has very courteously lent me the proof sheets of a valuable paper which he read before the Society of Antiquaries upon the Classification of Mappæ Mundi.

BEAZLEY (C. Raymond). The Dawn of Modern Geography. 3 vols. *London*, 1897-1906.

Each volume has much the most valuable matter on early maps necessary to every student. Mr. Beazley supplemented what is in this great book by articles in the Geographical Society Journal in vols. 14, 15 and 16, on "New Light on some Mediæval Maps."

BEVAN (Rev. W. L.) and PHILLOTT (Rev. H. W.). Mediæval Geography. An Essay in illustration of the Hereford Mappa Mundi. *London*, 1873.

A full and interesting study of the great Hereford picture map.

CHUBB (T). A Descriptive List of the Printed Maps of Somersetshire, 1575-1914. *Taunton*, 1914.

Mr. Chubb, who was for years head of the map department at the British Museum, here gives descriptive notes on all the maps of Somersetshire. One value this book has is that the information it contains relating to the county dealt with can be applied to any other county equally.

CROSS (W. Redmond). Dutch Cartographers of the Seventeenth Century. (Geographical Review, vol. 6, July, 1918).

DALY (Charles P.) On the early history of Cartography, or what we know of maps and map-making before the time of Mercator. (Journal of the American Geog. Socy., vol. xi., 1879).

Possibly the best general account of early cartography, containing the knowledge of a lifetime. The article is fully illustrated with reproductions of the earliest maps.

FORDHAM (Sir [Herbert] George). Studies in Carto-Bibliography, British and French. *Oxford*, 1914.

Sir George Fordham was one of the first to stimulate an interest in the study of old maps. The above volume, a book of under two hundred pages, contains a great body of most valuable information from first-hand study of maps and atlases. The chapters upon the study of the cartography of the English and Welsh Counties and that upon the Cartography of the Provinces of France, 1570-1757, are by far the best that have been written.

FORDHAM (Sir [Herbert] George). An Address on the Evolution of the maps of the British Isles delivered at Manchester, January 26th, 1923. *Manchester*, 1923.

An excellent brief and condensed statement of English County maps.

HALL (Elial F.). Gerard Mercator, his life and works. (Journal of the American Geographical Society. Volume 10, 1878).

A valuable paper.

JOMARD (E.F.) Les Monuments de la Géographie. *Paris*, 1854-1862.

A great facsimile atlas. A list of the maps comprised is given in Phillips, i. pp. 71-73.

KEANE (John). The Evolution of Geography. *London*, 1899.

A most excellent epitome with a chapter upon Early and Mediæval Maps.

MARTIN (William), M.A., LL.D., F.S.A. Early maps of London. (Papers contributed to the London and Middlesex Archæological Society, 1916-1920).

——— The Interpretation of Maps of the 16th. and 17th. centuries. (South Eastern Naturalist, 1910).

The above papers crystallize in a small compass a mass of information not obtainable elsewhere. Dr. Martin's studies are indispensable to all map students. I have found them of the utmost value.

MILLER (K.) Mappæ Mundi: die ältesten Weltkarten. 6 vols. *Stuttgart,* 1895-98.

A list of maps reproduced is given in Phillips, i. 74-75.

NORDENSKIÖLD (A.E.). Facsimile atlas to the early history of cartography. 51 facsimile maps. Folio. *Stockholm,* 1889.

Valuable for Ptolemy and early charts. A list of the facsimiles is given in Phillips, i. pp. 75-76.

PHILLIPS (Philip Lee). A List of Geographical Atlases in the Library of Congress with Bibliographical notes. 4 vols. *Washington,* 1909-1920.

The most essential work for the study of old maps. The Library of Congress has a very fine collection of Atlases and has issued this magnificent catalogue to assist students. The British Museum and other libraries may well do the same. I have made constant use of Mr. Phillips's great book.

SANTAREM (Vicomte de). Essai sur l'histoire de la cosmographie et de la cartographie pendant le moyen age, etc. 3 vols., *Paris,* 1849-52.

A valuable Atlas reproducing the most famous mediæval maps. A list of the maps contained in this great book is given in Phillips, i. pp. 81-86.

STEVENSON (Edward Luther). Willem Janszoon Blaeu, 1571-1638. A sketch of his life and work. *New York,* 1914.

While we await a good monograph upon the Dutch Cartographers, the above excellent volume remains by far the best account of Blaeu. It is based upon Baudet's book issued at Utrecht in 1871.

STEVENSON (Edward Luther). Portolan Charts. *New York,* Hispanic Society of America.

THACHER (Joseph Boyd). The Continent of America: its discovery and its baptism. An essay on the nomenclature of the old continents. A critical and bibliographical inquiry into the naming of America, and into the growth of the cosmography of the New World, etc., pp. xvii., 270; 4 pl., 1 port., 2 facs., 19 maps. 4° *New York.* W. E. Benjamin, 1896.

A most valuable and interesting addition to the bibliography of cartography. Chapter II. contains "Cartography of the World." Facing p. 195 is the map of Juan de la Cosa, drawn about 1500 on ox-hide, and at the end "A series of fourteen maps, from 1478 to 1570, showing the growth of the geographical knowledge of the New World."

WINSOR (Justin). Atlases of the Seventeenth Century. (See his Narrative and Critical History of America, volume 4).

Valuable.

WINSOR (Justin). A Bibliography of Ptolemy's Geography. (In Harvard University Bulletin, No. 24, 1883 and onwards).

CURRENT GENERAL READING

BAGROW (Leo) History of Cartography. Ed. R.A. Skelton Second edition, enlarged. Chicago, 1985.

BAYNTON-WILLIAMS (R.H.) Investing in Maps. London, 1969.

BOOTH (John) Looking at Old Maps. Westbury, 1979.

BROWN (Lloyd) The Story of Maps. London, 1951.

CAMPBELL (Tony) Early Maps. New York, 1981.

CHILD (Heather) Decorative Maps. London, 1956.

CRONE (G.R.) Maps and Their Makers: An Introduction to the History of Cartography. Revised Edition. London, 1979.

GOHM (Douglas) Antique Maps of Europe, the Americas, West Indies, Australasia, Africa, the Orient. London, 1972.

GOHM (Richard van der) Antique Maps For the Collector. Edinburgh, 1972.

HARLEY (J.B.) & WOODWARD (David) The History of Cartography. Volume 1: Cartography in Prehistoric, Ancient and Medieval Europe and the Mediterranean. Further volumes to come. Chicago, 1987.

HARVEY (P.D.A.) The History of Topographical Maps, Symbols, Pictures and Surveys. Folkestone, 1980.

HODGKISS (Alan) Understanding Maps: A Systematic History of Their Use and Development. London, 1981.

I.M.: IMAGO MUNDI The Journal of the International Society for the History of Cartography. Continuing series.

JOURDIN (Michel Mollat) & RONCIERE (Monique de) Sea Charts of the Early Explorers: 13th to 17th Century. New York, 1984.

LISTER, R. Antique Maps and their Cartographers. London, 1970.

LISTER, R. How To Identify Old Maps and Globes. London, 1965. Also issued as Old Maps and Globes, London, 1979.

THE MAP COLLECTORS' SERIES now discontinued series of 110 monographs on particular aspects of Map-making.

MORELAND (Carl) & BANNISTER (David) Antique Maps: A Collector's Handbook. London, 1983.

NORDENSKIOLD (A.E.) Facsimile Atlas of the History of Cartography. Reprint edition. New York, 1973.

NORDENSKIOLD (A.E.) Periplus: An Essay on The Early History of Charts and Sailing Directions. Stockholm, 1897.
POTTER (Jonathan) Country Life Book of Antique Maps: An Introduction to the History of Maps and How to Appreciate Them. London, 1988.
PUTMAN (R.) Early Sea Charts. New York, 1983.
SKELTON (R.A.) Explorer's Maps. Third Edition. London, 1970.
T.M.C.: THE MAP COLLECTOR Quarterly journal, December 1979.
TOOLEY (R.V.) Maps and Map-makers. Seventh Edition. London, 1987.
TOOLEY (R.V.C.), BRICKER & CRONE (G.R.) Landmarks of Mapmaking. An Illustrated Survey of Maps and Map-Makers. Amsterdam, 1968. Also issued as A History of Cartography.
WOODWARD (David) Five Centuries of Map Printing. Chicago, 1975.